Praise for

# SELL LIKE A SPY

"'Your most powerful weapon is your mind!' an Army Special Forces recruiting poster from the late '60s proclaimed. That remains true today because no matter what weapons special forces soldiers employ, they must have the ability to build and establish trust and rapport with foreign partners around the world, men and women of often vastly different cultures, languages, and histories. As readers of *Sell Like a Spy* will find, they can learn and absorb the same principles and ways of thinking from the special forces that results in operational success in our environment, to apply to the world you live and work in."

—LIEUTENANT GENERAL JOHN F. MULHOLLAND JR. (RET.),
former Deputy Commander of the United
States Special Operations Command

"In *Sell Like a Spy*, Jeremy Hurewitz does an excellent job of identifying best practices in information gathering, understanding people, and assessing situations from people with decades of experience honing these skills in the intelligence and law enforcement world. He shares with the reader how to use these skill sets to succeed in all sorts of aspects of their lives. A useful and fascinating read for just about anyone."

—MARK SULLIVAN, former Director of the Secret Service

"In *Sell Like a Spy*, Jeremy Hurewitz has given us a unique and intriguing look into the communication- and relationship-building skills used by FBI hostage negotiators to gain a peaceful surrender, by criminal interrogators in gaining cooperation, and by CIA case officers when recruiting spies. Viewed from his background in journalism and business consulting, Hurewitz explains how these highly effective methods can be used more broadly in the business world to achieve success. A well-written, great read that I highly recommend."

—GARY NOESNER, former FBI Chief Hostage Negotiator, and author
of *Stalling for Time: My Life as an FBI Hostage Negotiator*

"We'd like to think of spycraft as all cloak-and-dagger work in the shadows. But Jeremy Hurewitz, in this remarkable new book, shows that the best spies are really elite salespeople at heart. They can connect with, well, just about anyone. Having had remarkable access to top spies through a career in corporate security, Jeremy reveals the secrets they used to succeed. Not surprisingly, if you can sell while deeply undercover you can sell just about anything—and the lessons in this book will serve anyone working in corporate America today."

—PAUL SULLIVAN, former *New York Times* columnist,
author of *Clutch: Excel Under Pressure*, and
Founder of The Company of Dads

"Jeremy Hurewitz knows what good intelligence officers know: when it comes to closing deals, creativity matters. He shows that throughout his engrossing new book, *Sell Like a Spy*, which puts the reader in a position to learn real spy tradecraft to connect more deeply and influence people in their lives. His book is a page-turner, with real-life examples of how spies have used these techniques for generations. An essential read for anyone interested in broadening their social skills."

—JUVAL AVIV, former Mossad officer,
Founder of Interfor Inc., and author of
*Staying Safe: The Complete Guide to Protecting
Yourself, Your Family, and Your Business*

"Jeremy Hurewitz spent years working side-by-side with CIA case officers, FBI agents, and other government officials. With *Sell Like a Spy*, he taps that unique experience to provide crucial insights that can help businesspeople develop relationships, collect information, and overcome challenges."

—GREGORY ZUCKERMAN, Special Writer, *The Wall Street Journal*,
and *New York Times* bestselling author of *The Man Who Solved
the Market: How Jim Simons Launched the Quant Revolution*

"*Sell Like a Spy* is flat-out a great read and an innovative playbook—really a master class for serious sales professionals looking to up their game and become elite in their field. Ubiquitous information, macro forces, and competition make selling harder than ever with every pipeline opportunity a mission and every negotiation a complex operation. Jeremy Hurewitz does a brilliant job tapping into the clandestine world of espionage to extract unique best practices, leverage proven techniques by arguably the world's best sellers—SPIES—to give any sales professional willing to invest in their craft a serious competitive edge."

—PAT DONEGAN, former Senior Managing Director of Sales
Excellence, The Riverside Company

"The lessons of espionage directly relate to sales: it all comes down to the art of human persuasion. That's why this book is so useful and fascinating, because modern sales teams can adopt practices that have been employed by governments for years. . . . And not in a nefarious way, but in a way that actually builds trust. *Sell Like a Spy* is a great read and a lot of fun!"

—SAM JACOBS, CEO & Founder of Pavilion,
and *Wall Street Journal* bestselling author of
*Kind Folks Finish First: The Considerate Path
to Success in Business and Life*

# SELL
# LIKE A
# SPY

## THE ART OF PERSUASION FROM THE WORLD OF ESPIONAGE

## JEREMY HUREWITZ

*Foreword by Robert Grenier,*
*Former Director of the CIA National Counterterrorism Center*

DIVERSION
BOOKS
NEW YORK

Diversion Books
A division of Diversion Publishing Corp.
www.diversionbooks.com

For more information, email info@diversionbooks.com

First Diversion Books Edition: August 2024
Hardcover ISBN: 9781635769937
e-ISBN: 9781635769210

Design by Neuwirth & Associates
Printed in the United States of America

10  9  8  7  6  5  4  3  2  1

Diversion books are available at special discounts for bulk purchases
in the US by corporations, institutions, and other organizations.
For more information, please contact admin@diversionbooks.com.

*To Rachel, for all that's been and all that's to come.*

# CONTENTS

# FOREWORD

*by Robert L. Grenier,*
*Former Director of the CIA National*
*Counterterrorism Center*

Throughout my career in the Central Intelligence Agency, I had
to persuade foreigners to work with the U.S. government—to sell
them, if you will, on the idea and why it made sense for them to
agree to cooperate.

The most extreme example came in the days immediately
following 9/11, when I was serving as station chief in Islamabad,
Pakistan, and journeyed to the dusty provincial desert outpost
of Quetta, in the southern part of Pakistan, to meet with Mullah
Akhtar Mohammad Osmani, the number-two leader in the
Taliban. I was the first U.S. government official to meet with a
member of the Taliban after 9/11, and my task was to persuade
Osmani to turn over Osama bin Laden before the U.S. was forced
to go to war with him and his Taliban forces.

To say that the good mullah and I had little in common was to
vastly understate the case. I was from the Eastern (U.S.) establish-
ment, a product of boarding schools and the Ivy League, someone
from the intelligence world for whom broad open-mindedness
toward foreign cultures and alternative ways of thinking was both
a personal instinct and a professional necessity. Despite what
Hollywood tells you about the life of spies, in my experience
aggression was generally confined to the tennis court.

Mullah Osmani, conversely, was a grizzled veteran of over twenty years of primitive, pitiless war. A bearlike tribal commander, with a huge black turban and a copious beard, his violent world was bounded by a narrow conception of fundamentalist Islam. Although he had no personal love for bin Laden, he could not ignore the fact that the Saudi was a religious hero and a champion to his own people, and that to hand him over would be considered a great betrayal by virtually everyone whose opinion mattered to him. His instinctive response to U.S. demands was violent defiance. At the same time, however, war was no abstraction to him, and the prospect of yet more hostilities, this time with a superpower of unimaginable military prowess, was something he fervently wanted to avoid.

During eight hours of conversation spread out over two days, we went around and around, with no discernible progress. I pitched myself as an impartial observer, earnestly trying to help Osmani find a way to avoid the American juggernaut while still satisfying the core requirements demanded by both sides. Again and again, I proposed face-saving ways for the Afghans to meet the American president's demands to avoid war, only to run up against the mullah's narrow lack of imagination. Still, his growing agitation at the thought of yet another years-long war with a superpower was a strong selling point, and I played it judiciously, again and again, while making sure that the thinly veiled threat of U.S. punishment did not push him over into snarling, unthinking defiance.

The weight of this decision seemed to overwhelm him. He felt he was trapped between concessions he could not make and the unpalatable prospect of war with America. He was despairing. His shoulders hunched and his body slumping in his chair, I could see him literally shrink before me. But those eight previous hours had had one clear effect: he had become convinced of my sincerity in wanting to help him. He knew I understood both him and his situation. Against all odds, I had become his friend.

Looking up at me, he said the words I had hoped for: "Tell me what I should do."

Without any hesitation, I mapped the way out. I explained how his boss, Mullah Omar, had created a trap for himself and his country, and how only Mullah Osmani could save them. Step by step, I explained how he needed to place Mullah Omar under house arrest, seize control of the capital, consolidate his support among the other senior commanders, and announce the steps he was taking to bring bin Laden to Islamic justice and to save Afghanistan from the fate to which Mullah Omar had condemned it.

It was as though I had thrown a line to a drowning man. Leaping to his feet, Osmani seized it. "I will do it!" he cried, as he wrapped me in a bear hug. We ate a hearty lunch together and, after hugging me again, Osmani mounted his heavily armed motorcade and roared off back to Afghanistan. I felt the deal was done—and, with a nod to this book, that the sale had been made.

Alas, it was not to be. As I feared, Osmani's resolve did not survive the bumpy, six-hour drive to Kandahar, Afghanistan. What I didn't know then was that while I seemed to have sold Osmani, he had no hope of selling his fellow commanders on the idea to follow him, rather than the charismatic Mullah Omar. After the euphoria prompted by our conversation had faded, he must have come to his senses.

This story would be far more compelling if it reflected a success. If this long conversation had resolved the impasse between the U.S. and the Taliban, avoiding what we now know would be twenty years of warfare and much death and destruction, we'd see it differently.

But the point of the story is that despite the hopelessness of the situation, despite the vast, ultimately unbridgeable gap between

Osmani and me, patience, understanding, and genuine empathy brought us to a point where, despite all odds, we agreed on a joint course of action. I had made the sale; but as any salesperson will likely have experienced, sometimes things can still go wrong after you've convinced your counterparty of the merits of your pitch.

Among the most critical abilities of the spy, or anyone whose livelihood depends on influencing others, is a capacity for empathy. It is by putting yourself in the shoes of another, understanding the context in which their decisions are made, that one can begin to imagine the circumstances under which they might take the actions you wish for, even if that would take them far from where they had been when you started with them.

Imagine what similar techniques could render in the case of a sales process, with so many more advantages on your side, and so many fewer obstacles? That is the benefit, and the promise of this book.

When Jeremy Hurewitz approached me with the idea for *Sell Like a Spy* I was instantly intrigued and quickly grasped how compelling the concept was. In a series of conversations, I shared some of my experiences from a long career in espionage, as well as many of the broad lessons in human behavior that I had drawn from that life. Espionage, as anyone from that world will tell you, is after all a human business. Its field of endeavor is the palette of human character.

Subsequently, Jeremy also drew on the experiences of others, former colleagues of mine as well as members of the military and law enforcement, who added their own insights. They, too, often work in the battle space of the human psyche.

It was up to Jeremy, whose experiences straddle the worlds of journalism, corporate investigations, and national security policy, as well as sales, to distill these aggregate lessons and to apply them to the world of sales. Corporate sales may seldom be thought of in the same context as intelligence, law enforcement, and military operations; but, like those, it is a people business, and the ability to influence others to move in an intended direction is the key to success.

For myself, I cannot pretend to understand the commercial sales world, but the professional corporate salesperson is very likely to be able to take the lessons drawn from spy operations and apply them, by analogy, to their own context and alternative purposes. That is the process that Jeremy has been able so skillfully to facilitate.

# INTRODUCTION

Natalie* was a highly trained CIA case officer with a roster of techniques that she used to connect with targets. A Muslim of Lebanese heritage, she utilized her knowledge of Islam to establish ties with terrorist targets and remove them from the battlefield.

But this mission was a bit different. Natalie wouldn't be chatting up someone at a teahouse or charming a foreign diplomat whose government might be covertly supporting a terror group. On this particular mission, she would be sitting in front of a computer screen.

The CIA had gathered intelligence that a top Yemen-based Al Qaeda lieutenant—we'll call him "Nabil"—was looking for a wife. The Agency managed to connect Natalie with him online, and they started corresponding. Her mission was to elicit Al Qaeda-insider information and, if at all possible, to get him to share details about himself that might help the CIA to target him.

Natalie, posing as Elmedina, slowly built rapport with Nabil, telling him of her life in Syria, the challenges she and her family had endured in the country's civil war, and how she was looking for a righteous man of faith to help her move forward with her life. She started the conversations warily, acting as if she were shy. But Nabil was interested, and he started pursuing Elmedina. She turned his interest against him, subtly getting him to share details that the Agency began to assemble into a broader picture.

---

* Names with an asterisk next to them have been sanitized to protect the identity of the intelligence officer.

The details Nabil shared about his life put him in Hadramawt Province, a terrorist stronghold in this desperately poor country. He mentioned certain roads and markets in nearby towns. He told his charming Elmedina that he traveled in a small Suzuki truck because the Americans tended to look for Toyota Hilux trucks. Critically, he noted that he had been injured in a recent skirmish and his leg was broken.

The CIA sent drones into the area they believed Nabil inhabited. Not long afterward, they spotted a Suzuki 4X4 and saw a man getting out of the passenger seat to head into an internet café. He made his way into the café with the help of crutches.

Nabil probably believed he was using good tradecraft, riding in a car that wasn't typical of his Al Qaeda colleagues. Perhaps he thought that patronizing an internet café would avoid the chance of his compound being compromised because it provided a degree of cover from his enemy's electronic surveillance efforts.

But Elmedina's tradecraft was better. She chatted with him over the internet while he was in the café, ramping up her virtual affection for him, telling him that she longed for a time soon when she could meet him in person, when they could be together.

Eventually, Nabil said he had to go. He hobbled back to his driver outside the internet café, perhaps enthusing over his potential bride-to-be, when soon after driving away from the café a missile from a Predator drone struck his truck, obliterating the vehicle and completing the mission of removing Nabil from the battlefield.

Elmedina's proficiency in subtly collecting bits of information* helped her contribute to the mission of removing a notorious terrorist with the blood of civilians on his hands.

Later on, Natalie briefed a top CIA official about the operation. He was amazed that the CIA—virtually, using a false persona—was

---

* Elmedina used the skill of "elicitation" to achieve her mission. We will soon see how effective this tactic can be in a business setting as well.

able to elicit the kind of information that led to a successful kinetic strike. "This is the way of the future," he commented.

Rick* was a CIA case officer with a very particular set of skills. For one, he was an expert skier. A former teenage ski-racing champion from the Rocky Mountains, Rick always looked for opportunities to hit the slopes during his Agency tours overseas—not to compete anymore, but to connect with people and feel tied to his upbringing despite his rootless lifestyle. Most of all, he just really loved to ski.

Rick never saw his passion for skiing as a potential tool in accomplishing the primary aspect of his job—the recruitment of foreign agents to collect intelligence for the U.S. government. Then again, maybe subconsciously he always had—spies know that utilizing any aspect of their personality to connect with their targets is just good practice. But would Rick have guessed that skiing would help him enlist the most valuable recruits of his career?

It was the early 1990s; the Cold War had recently ended; and while the rest of the world was enjoying the peace dividend, the CIA was still hard at work, focused on the challenges that Russia presented to U.S. foreign policy. It was essentially the assignment that U.S. spooks had been working on for decades—trying to understand the Russians. But it was no longer about understanding advances in the Soviet military arsenal or countering the influence of Communism around the world. At this turning point in history, it was about understanding the state of the Russian government and whether Boris Yeltsin would be pushed out by revanchist elements from the ultra-left or extremist right-wing nationalists. The CIA was concerned about the safety and security of nuclear weapons in the

---

* Rick was operating under diplomatic cover.

Russian Federation, too, and whether Russian nuclear scientists were making their nuclear expertise available to the highest bidder in the global underground of terrorists and rogue states.

Rick was based in the Central Asian nation of Tajikistan and was tasked with recruiting Russian diplomats to gain insight into what was happening in that fractious country.

The problem he faced was that the Russian diplomats based in Dushanbe—the capital of Tajikistan—seemingly hadn't gotten the memo that the Cold War had ended. The U.S. government was a friend now, right? Well, these diplomats still operated under rules that prohibited them from meeting alone with U.S. counterparts.

So what did Rick do? He went skiing.

Rick knew that Russians are avid mountaineers, and he bet that if he hit the ski slopes in that impoverished Central Asian nation (even if they were just rudimentary slopes), he would bump into Russians, possibly some recruitment targets.

That's exactly what happened. Rick's passionate, skillful skiing impressed, and he quickly made friends on the slopes. Just as he'd planned, these new pals included Russians with information and insights that were extremely valuable to the U.S. government.

Rick was able to make his particular kind of sale—persuading his target to commit treason—by following his passion and by going to where his very particular clients might be. Those of us in sales can think the same way and get the same results. It's just one of the many ways that we can all sell like a spy.*

Spies have intrigued us for generations. From the Cold War image of a mysterious figure in a fedora and trench coat lurking under a fog-shrouded streetlamp, to the dashing James Bond character

---

* We'll discuss later in the book how Rick was using techniques I will refer to as "superpowers" and "going to where the clients are."

saving the world from peril, to the nearly superhero level of Jason Bourne's augmented skills, we are fascinated by the danger and glamor of espionage.

Pop culture has given us a memorable cast of characters that have the ability to become nearly invisible, collect the information they need, and defeat the bad guys.

The truth, of course, is quite a bit different. Spies do leverage some extraordinary skills to do their work. But they are very much human beings, and the work they do is in large part far more mundane than Hollywood would lead us to believe. While it's true that spies are trained to deal with dangerous situations, for the most part their work involves influencing people, developing their targets in order to understand what will motivate them to cooperate, and ultimately recruiting agents to collect intelligence for the U.S. government.

So, could it be that spies are actually the world's best salespeople? After all, what is a harder sale to make than getting someone to commit treason?

I have been mistaken for a spy, but I have never actually been one. At least not one working for any government. During nearly a decade abroad as a journalist, I was sometimes accused of being with the CIA—and there was a girlfriend or two who teased me about their suspicions because of my travel schedule—but there was no truth to it. I have some skills that are helpful in espionage—good at eliciting information, a natural ability to develop relationships—but I also wear my heart on my sleeve and I'm better at keeping the secrets of others than my own.

If I look back on my time overseas as a journalist, I reflect on moments as a naïve young journalist excited to be at embassy functions in international cities. I remember being flattered to have diplomats at these functions ask me questions and feign interest in my point of view. Because of my work at the time, I was speaking regularly with editors of influential newspapers around the world, with well-known academics, and often with leading politicians. When I look back on these moments, I see spies with diplomatic cover using flattery to elicit information and using their great listening skills to get me to open up about everything I had learned. I was never the wiser for it, because techniques like "the violin conversation" and "active listening" had me believing that we were just having normal conversations. In reality, they were expertly drawing out information, assessing who I was, and determining whether I could be valuable to them in any broader sense.

Much of my work as a journalist involved writing about security and intelligence, and I've always had an interest in, and read widely about, espionage. Indeed, part of the reason I was drawn to the corporate security industry was to get closer to the former intelligence officers, law enforcement, special forces, and other government officials who populate the industry so I could learn about them—and from them.

And learn I did.

Let me tell you how I came to be a corporate spy and work with former intelligence officers and a variety of other former government officials. But before I let you in on the secrets of selling like a spy, let me share some details about the shadowy world of corporate security and how I found a place in it.

## CORPORATE SECURITY

We could go back through time and find numerous examples of "corporate security," especially if we take an expansive view and include the world of mercenaries. Some of my employers had corporate divisions that were military contractors, and I'll speak to that. We could also look back to the Pinkerton agency and its detectives and strike-busters for a corporate security lineage. But for our purposes, let's focus on recent history.

Most people credit the origins of the modern corporate-security industry to Kroll Associates. Established by the legendary Jules Kroll, a former federal prosecutor, he surveyed the business landscape of the early 1970s and realized that the business world could use some of what traditional private investigators did. But those services would need to avoid the tawdry aspects of private investigator work so famously showcased in pulp fiction and noir cinema. He was highly successful in professionalizing this industry, essentially creating it out of whole cloth. Just as "getting a Xerox" used to mean making a document copy and "Googling" something means searching for it online, ordering a Kroll report was for years the byword for ordering a background check.

The industry expanded throughout the '70s and '80s, but the end of the Cold War proved to be a major catalyst for growth. With the Iron Curtain coming down, countries with centrally planned economies were now reforming and opening up their financial systems, embracing capitalism. This created enormous opportunities for corporations and investors eager to leverage the peace dividend of the era to enter new markets and participate in their rapid economic growth.

But all opportunity comes with risk, and there was certainly plenty of that. Many of these newly open countries teetered on the edge of chaos as the Soviet Union removed decades of foreign aid, creating power vacuums filled by warlords, criminals, and other power-hungry players. In places like Eastern Europe, the privatization of industry in the '90s was plagued by corruption, creating a whole class of sketchy oligarchs that Western businesses eyed warily when it came to establishing partnerships.

The corporate-security industry grew rapidly, helping these corporations and investors manage and mitigate these types of security risks. It helped these groups to understand the variety of players operating in these newly opened markets, and helped ensure the safety of businesspeople traveling to these dangerous regions.

To build the specific labor force it needed to mitigate the very particular risks its clients faced, the industry hired former government employees. They brought knowledge of these emerging markets, real experience with violent groups and situations, and other important skills and expertise.

What started as managing physical and reputational risk security has blossomed into a vibrant industry. Corporate security now includes a wide spectrum of services like business-continuity planning, crisis management, asset tracing, litigation support, political-risk advice, cybersecurity, and even e-discovery.

While the industry particularly values the experience of those with government backgrounds, former journalists are also welcome. Journalists bring talent for turning phrases; investigative experience; and, in many cases (mine included), coveted experience in some of the emerging markets that clients are deeply interested and invested in.

So when I came home from China after my decade abroad, open to the possibility of leaving the media world and wondering about where my skill set and experience might fit in, I was pointed to the corporate-security industry. I joined a global risk consultancy, a prestigious British firm who had been a player in the space almost as long as Kroll.

Hired on to a hybrid team that did project management as well as business development, I needed to be credible to clients regarding the wide suite of services this firm employed, and also to have the ability to grow relationships with those same clients.

I audited courses on kidnap-for-ransom cases—an all-too-common issue for international businesses and organizations—and learned all about this fascinating subset of the industry; I collaborated closely with our political-risks analysts—a team of dozens spread around the world with particular expertise on certain countries or regions—to write risk reports for our clients who were considering entering a particular country and seeking to understand how an upcoming election might impact their industry. I also worked with specialists to help businesses plan for the outcome of a major hurricane, earthquake, or terrorist attack.

The biggest stretch for me, and some of the most colorful work, was to manage executive protection details. I established a relationship with one of the biggest global consultancies, who hired us to protect their teams working in Iraq. Every other week, their consultants were flying into Baghdad and then heading to the southern Iraqi oil fields, and we picked them up at the airport (after their planes did the famous nose-dive into the airport to avoid rocket attacks from insurgents) and then transported them, with an extra security car in the rear in case the first car was attacked.

I once managed the security detail of one of the world's most well-known hedge-fund investors. He was going on a cruise down the Nile with some of his billionaire buddies, and we had a security team on the yacht as well as a follow-car along the bank. Our political-risk team was picking up the signs of incipient unrest in Egypt—riots on bread lines in major cities—and we recommended augmenting the security detail to have a second follow car on the bank on the other side of the Nile as well.

The client firm was well known for its culture of "radical transparency," and so it wasn't a huge surprise when the Chief Security Officer (CSO) called me back after hearing the firm's recommendation from me. He chewed me out and accused me of trying to upsell them and demanded to speak to my boss. The head of our

New York office was a dapper former FBI agent, and he adroitly mollified the CSO (a former SEAL, if I recall correctly), and they agreed on the expanded security detail.

The trip went off without any incidents, but a few weeks afterward the Arab Spring erupted in Tunisia and quickly spread to Egypt. I remember touching base with that CSO around that time, following up on potential future work, and contextualizing the situation in Egypt while being careful not to hold it over him that we had been right. It was an important lesson for me on dealing with a difficult client and the power of the information we had as we made crucial, potentially life-and-death recommendations to our clients.

Another unforgettable learning experience was when our CEO shared a story about an Iraq-based project that we declined. It showcased our professionalism and how different we were from the cowboys at Blackwater—a firm that was attracting media attention in the late 2000s for a series of high-profile mishaps where their trigger-happy employees were accused of massacring civilians.

Our CEO pointed to the infamous "Fallujah ambush" of Blackwater's employees being killed, burned, and strung up from a bridge in that Iraqi city, a hotbed of insurgency that would become a major battleground between U.S. forces and Islamic extremists.

We had been asked by a client of ours to provide security for their logistics in Iraq. Our Iraq country manager objected to the route the client wanted to take and said it had to be done differently, a more circuitous route that would take more time and cost the client more money, but, in his informed view, one that would be much safer. The client refused to reconsider their plans; and when we declined the project because we felt it was too risky, they went with Blackwater and the world could see the results.

The organization I was working for had unique expertise within the business world, expertise that was to be heeded in order to avoid serious, life-threatening problems. I saw how high-performing management teams looked out for their employees, trusted those employees and their knowledge in the field, and gave a surprising role to ethical guidelines that mandate sticking to missions and mindsets.

But the work I focused on more than anything was investigations, and that put me side by side with CIA case officers frequently. This work was reputational due diligence, often called background investigations. For example, if a private-equity firm is acquiring a company, looking into the backgrounds of the founder and the top members of the team is an industry best practice.

The work is crucial because while the investor might have spent a lot of time with the founder and their team, what you see might not be what you get. If you're going to invest $100 million into a company, you'll want to know if there are any skeletons in the closet.

So we would quietly dig in on these cases, building our approach off of what the public-records research—phase one in any investigation—showed us. If that founder had two DUI cases in the span of three years just under a decade ago, we'd make it a point to find out about it. Are they a problem drinker to this day? Or was this a particularly difficult period in their life (maybe they were going through a divorce or having problems with a child) and they have put this behind them? What do former employees say when contacted and asked about their leadership style, their ethical sense? These qualitative insights have huge value, and smart investors and executives know not to cut corners when making deals.

Background investigation is one of the areas where I really saw the skills that case officers leverage in action. I was enamored with the planning they did, simply for the approach toward potential sources, trying to anticipate what they might think, whether they would be reluctant to talk, how to make them feel comfortable when asked about sensitive matters. Sometimes it wouldn't work and the source wouldn't speak. But more often than not it would, and we're going to talk about some of those methods of getting people to open up to you.

Occasionally we would go even deeper. Perhaps the target of the investigation was a big tennis player who played regularly at their country club. We might find a way into that country club and observe them playing a few matches. Do they smash their racket when they make a mistake or lose a set? Are they gracious in defeat, or do they sulk and act like a jerk? These character traits could provide insights into how this executive will react to setbacks in the corporate world, and they are highly valuable to the smart investor looking for any sort of edge or insight when putting a lot of money on the table.

There have always been gray areas of the corporate-security industry. Let's face it, so much of this work demands working around the ethical edges.

On investigations, most of the firms I've worked for would avoid pretexting, or essentially lying to a source about who they are and why they are asking questions. Most firms hire subcontractors to do the source work, to provide a proxy between the firm and the project. We would hire people for whom it would make sense to ask the questions we needed answers to. Sometimes that meant hiring someone who worked as a headhunter to call people and ask about an executive's background. Other times it meant hiring a freelance journalist, perhaps one who covered a particular industry (say, healthcare), to ask about details involving a particular situation that a hedge-fund client wanted to understand more deeply.

Each firm I've worked for is a little different, as is each situation. Some firms feel it's okay to occasionally raid someone's garbage to find information on them because it's legal in that particular state and could yield important intelligence. I've never wanted to be involved with digging through garbage, and have avoided such projects and the firms that engage in that practice. But it is certainly an industry that has a way of creeping into ethical gray areas.

Executing for clients in the different areas of support we provided allowed me to learn firsthand from former spies and other ex-government officials. But just as important was spending time with these people, getting to know how each of them approached relationship development, the collection of information, and how to overcome challenges. The way each individual personalized the training they had was one of the most important lessons about how to be effective in using the methods I will describe in this book.

There was a particularly unassuming former case officer, for instance, a lapsed Mormon, who showed the importance of "active listening"—one of the main reasons I came to feel that this particular skill is the most important that any spy or salesperson could have. This case officer had a way of getting you to talk, of pushing the spotlight off himself and back on to you. It was his quiet tone of voice, his seemingly shy nature and deference in conversation that led you to feel he was non-threatening, trustworthy, on your side. I watched while over several years he assumed larger and larger roles at our firm, his self-effacing façade hiding someone who was really a canny and ambitious operator.

Another former case officer's cover wasn't fully rolled back; he neither advertised nor hid his Agency background. A veteran of some of the roughest CIA stations in the 2000s during America's "war on terror," an accomplished triathlete, he stood out to me with his humble nature. Not as self-effacing as the previously described spy, this guy had a gregarious personality, but it wasn't about drawing attention to himself, and it certainly wasn't trying to traffic on what was an accomplished CIA career. His humility was inspiring and remains so.

A military sniper introduced me to his world of moral ambiguity and how he now managed executive-protection tasks for some of the world's most well-known businesspeople. Though he wasn't physically imposing, he had an off-putting way about him because of his taciturn nature, especially once you learned what he had done in the military. But I knew he held interesting knowledge and made it a point to get to know him, learning how his calm persona was essential to the task of spending long hours looking through the lens of a sniper scope. I learned how important it is to have an intense focus on the mission, how essential it is to block everything else out, including the natural human sympathy that forms when someone is observed closely in mundane activity even though you will have to pull the trigger at a certain moment. He taught me how he used the same sort of steely focus when he was protecting an executive on a trip, and we discussed ways that this singular focus can help in every aspect of life.

The world of corporate security was in many ways like going to graduate school—a survey course of varied government trainings mixed into the bouillabaisse of global business. Synthesizing the lessons from an alphabet soup of government agencies, I developed *Sell Like a Spy* to share with you the lessons from these extraordinary public servants.

So, that's corporate security in a nutshell, and a bit of insight into some of the basics of corporate security tactics. But we need to go deeper to see the sales aspect of selling like a spy.

Throughout my career, a common theme has involved wearing several hats at once. I've always had something of a hybrid role— half practitioner, half sales. That's a perch I've always felt comfortable on, and one that I think is a good place for anyone in sales to think about. We should all be essentially subject-matter experts in the particular product or service we are selling, shouldn't we?

I have a lineage in sales—my grandfather and father were both salespeople. My father leveraged his gregarious personality to build long-term, durable relationships with his clients, people I met because the relationships were so strong that our families would intermingle. My mother was a beloved educator, but critical to the success of her career was her winning personality, one in which people could detect her sincerity and her inherent likeability (which, we'll hear later on from a seasoned FBI agent, might be the most important personality trait to have). Many of the successes I've had in sales come from the personality traits my parents passed along to me.

At the heart of this book is a unique selling-and-spying career path that has fostered my ideas about connections and communications. It's time for me to share with you what I have learned. The skills I will describe are sometimes unconventional approaches that have helped me thrive not only in my career, but also in my everyday relationships.

I believe strongly that life is sales. Whether we work in sales or not, all of us are trying to influence others, get them to understand who we are, and build satisfying and deep relationships. The skills that make someone a good salesperson are often the same ones that allow that person to connect with people in their everyday lives. What I will share with you are skills that you can implement into your everyday life and, if utilized correctly, will help you be a better listener, improve your relationships, and prove useful in navigating this populous world.

# 1

# THE WORLD OF INTELLIGENCE

*Misconceptions, surprises, and the true work of spies*

James Bond is a farce, as much as Austin Powers is. Spies are not regulars at high-end casinos, with tuxedo-only wardrobes. They are not typically engaged in car chases and shootouts. If a spy is in that kind of situation, something has gone badly wrong.

The work of spies is developing and managing relationships, and so most of them—in their looks, their personalities, their backgrounds—are far from the James Bond archetype.

As one spy noted to me, they are typically *"medium everything"*— average height, looks, etc. Generally speaking, it's beneficial for a spy to be average-looking. Being able to blend into a room, materializing to make contact and ask a few questions, and then fading into the night is a good trait when it comes to espionage. Think about it—isn't that better for the work of a spy than being a heart-throb no one can take their eyes off of as they move around the room? That's why you're more likely to find a spy that looks like a frumpy academic than Daniel Craig.

That's not to say that there aren't attractive spies; of course there are, and I've met quite a few. But as a rule, put the James Bond or Jessica Chastain image out of your head.

Another misconception is that all spies are outgoing and gregarious. While it's true that most spies are similar to salespeople in that they tend to lean toward the extroverted side, just as I have worked with successful introverted salespeople, some spies are introverts. They tend to be self-deprecating, with a dark sense of humor, and they are great at getting people to open up. Among men, the subtle individual that doesn't try to out-Alpha the other person can often find themselves hearing the most valuable secrets. Introverts should note that it's easier for them to turn up their personality than to get an extrovert to turn theirs down (more later on amplifying or de-emphasizing aspects of your personality).

You might also be surprised to learn that the CIA recruits extensively from the Mormon community. Mormons are attractive recruitment targets for a few reasons: they typically do mission trips overseas when they're young, giving them the opportunity to learn to navigate different cultures and to pick up foreign languages; they come from cohesive, conservative, and patriotic communities, which helps when it comes to maintaining a focus on their mission, while making them easier to run background checks on during recruitment; and, as my former brash Aussie boss at a corporate security firm noted, "Less of a chance you'll find a photo of them snorting coke off a stripper's arse, mate."

## TERMINOLOGY

A few notes on spy terms.

What we tend to think of as a "spy" is actually known as a case officer. Case officers recruit agents, who they often think of as the actual spies because they're typically the ones stealing documents and taking the risks to get the intelligence. For our purposes, we'll play it a bit loose with the term "spy"; but, generally, when I use that term I'm referring to a CIA case officer.

Case officers work with analysts, who are generally working out of CIA headquarters in Langley, Virginia. They are usually country- or region-specific experts or have expertise on a certain sector (oil and gas, for instance) or a subject matter (say, Islam). They aid in the targeting process for prospective agents, and they contextualize the reporting from the field. Analysts help distill the raw intelligence collected from the field into a product shared with policymakers who use it to formulate national security policy.

There are essentially two types of case officers: those who operate under official cover, and those who do so under non-official cover. Non-official cover is often referred to by the acronym NOC, or other times as commercial cover officers.

Official cover generally means that you are ostensibly employed by the U.S. government. Typically, you are an employee of the State Department working out of a U.S. embassy or consulate abroad with a title like economic attaché or consular official. But really you are a CIA case officer looking to recruit and run foreign agents.

This is an important distinction, because if a person is caught engaged in espionage (or just breaking foreign laws), they might undergo some unpleasantness, and it will be an embarrassment to the local embassy or consulate, but the individual—because of their official government status—will typically just be kicked out of the country. The diplomatic term is *"persona non grata,"* often referred to as *"PNG'd"*—and this is a safeguard for all diplomats around the world. The next time you read about, say, the U.S. and Russia engaging in the tit-for-tat expulsion of diplomats, you can be sure that those being kicked out are spies operating under diplomatic cover.

Being a NOC is more dangerous and a bit rarer. A NOC has no overt relationship with the U.S. government. They typically have cover as a businessperson, sometimes with a well-known U.S.

company ostensibly employing them. These companies have quiet relationships with the U.S. government under which they will keep that person on the payroll, give them business cards, etc., but they don't actually work at that company. They are spies working overseas under that cover. Other times, the NOC will be employed by a tiny boutique firm that doesn't really exist, but the CIA provides the "back-office operations" should someone call the number on the card to check on the NOC's cover story.

If a NOC is caught, the U.S. government will do what they can for them, but they do not have the same courtesies extended to them as to the diplomats.

I worked extensively with one NOC in particular. He wasn't trained at the famed CIA facility known as The Farm, the CIA facility in rural Virginia where recruits typically undergo their intelligence training. He was trained separately, so only a handful of people at the CIA knew who he was. As part of his training he was given intensive Mandarin lessons, doing almost nothing else but studying the language for six months. Afterward, he was sent forth to recruit Chinese agents, leveraging the strong educational opportunities available in the U.S. as one tool to exploit the traditional preferences of Chinese parents to get their kids the best education possible as motivation to persuade them to cooperate with the CIA.

He led a secret life for years, with his parents as the only two people outside the Agency who knew his real job wasn't working for a private equity firm. Neither his siblings, his closest friends, nor even the girlfriend he was living with, who would become his wife, knew about his double life. When his fiancé found out about his true identity, she wasn't pleased, but the marriage plan survived.

I always admired this person's ability to connect with just about anyone we met, his incredibly wide range of conversational skills, and his innate ability to be able to turn on the charm or remain quiet and listen carefully as the situation called for. He was a true spy, one of the many I have learned from.

## CONNECTION

Talk to any former case officer about their work, and they will often tell you that their job resembled that of a psychiatrist. The hours of talking and bonding with an agent are not how Hollywood portrays it. In movies and TV shows, we often see spies coercing a target into supplying information. Whether it's blackmail or even torture, we're led to think that these heavy-handed methods are simply a part of the espionage tool kit.

I'm not going to say that coercion never happens; it absolutely does, especially among certain overseas intelligence agencies, in particular those from authoritarian countries unaccountable to civil society. The CIA certainly has some skeletons in their collective closets, and the enhanced interrogation scandals in the years after 9/11 are a very real black mark on the CIA, one the agency still reckons with.

But for the most part, the CIA is not training its case officers to blackmail their targets. It's been shown over and over again that information collected under duress is suspect—people will say whatever you want them to say if under enough pressure. And a person being blackmailed is not reliable and the relationship is usually short-lived.

John Sipher—a former Moscow station chief and head of the Russia desk at Langley—confirms that blackmail is used by the Russians and other intelligence agencies but "we don't use it. It's not just because of the moral side of things—it's because it doesn't work. If you blackmail or coerce, they always look for a way out, they despise you, and they're always looking for a chance to get out or double-cross you."

Hence a saying I've heard several times from case officers: "*Spies convince, thugs coerce.*"

Spies are looking to recruit agents—who they hope will gather information for the U.S. for a long time—by understanding what might *motivate* them to cooperate rather than *forcing* them to do so. Those motivations might be money, disillusionment with the authoritarian regime of their home country, the desire for educational opportunities available in the U.S. for their children, or any number of other reasons.

A former colleague of mine noted "Every good intelligence officer has a real bond with their target on some level and in some regard," and this has become my favorite quote to describe the work of spies, summing up what I admire so much about the skill set of these elite professionals. Rather than trying to coerce or blackmail, they spend weeks, months, sometimes even years cultivating a target, building rapport, establishing an emotional connection, before getting them to commit to gathering intelligence for the U.S. It is often a painstaking process, because they have to convince that person to betray their country, society, tribe, or sometimes even their families.

More from Sipher: "If someone is going to provide you with information that could be damaging to them, they have to trust you, trust that you understand your own system, and that you can keep them safe. You don't build trust without being yourself. I think most case officers would say the relationships they've developed with their agents are very real."

The successful case officer takes time to get to know their target, looking for emotional touchpoints, vulnerabilities, sensitive areas, and points on which they might establish a bond. Often the case officer has to bridge significant cultural distances. The CIA is astute when it comes to using certain case officers in certain situations and countries to exploit these cultural factors.

Sipher recalls how this training begins at The Farm for case officers, and how intellectual curiosity is at the heart of every successful case officer's tradecraft. "When I was going through The Farm as a student, I was hooked up with an older guy as part of a training exercise. It became clear that he was a deer hunter, that was his thing, but that's not my thing at all. It's not going to help me to say I have no interest in that, and I can't fake it completely and pretend I'm a hunter because he'll quickly understand that I don't know anything about it. But I can put myself in a position that the person will say 'hey, I'll take you and show you.' You have to be curious and interested in the world. You have to try to use pieces from your own life and tie it in to people and their lives. You don't have to pretend you're a scientist to speak with one, but you have to be interested in it to connect with that person."

*"I do not like that man, I need to get to know him better."*
—*Abraham Lincoln*

We've all encountered people who are enslaved to their own egos, their vision of themselves being uniquely intelligent and surrounded by idiots. Our strategies on how to deal with such people vary depending on our own personalities and the circumstances surrounding how we're interacting. Avoidance isn't a bad strategy— if you can choose to not deal with such a person, why bother?

But what if the key decision-maker on your potential sale is such a person? There are a few strategies from the world of espionage that can be helpful. Taking that Abraham Lincoln quote to heart and remembering the heroic efforts of case officers to bridge enormous cultural and personality gulfs can give you the inspiration to persevere beyond a difficult person to get to "yes."

Intelligence officers have to regularly deal with unpleasant and unsavory individuals. Think about the vast array of people that comprise a spy's recruitment pool. While a portion might be people they genuinely like and find interesting, a majority of them will not be individuals they would otherwise choose to spend time with. These include criminals, terrorists, and officials from some of the most oppressive and odious regimes around the world.

Whether it's the lowlife who wants money for prostitutes, or the disgruntled diplomat with a nasty axe to grind, a case officer has to find a way to build rapport with such targets and overcome their revulsion to spending time with morally base people.

When Marc Polymeropoulos—a twenty-six-year veteran of the CIA and one of its most decorated field officers—reflects on his time at the Agency, he doesn't miss his colleagues so much as the tight relationships he formed with agents. "I miss the agents, the people who took incredible risks; I miss the bond we had. Maybe it's just a brush pass* and understanding that brief interaction is so important that you actually have their life in your hands. Case officers always fall in love with our agents, and you know you have to turn over the agent to another case officer after a few years, because they need to be institutionalized by the Agency, particularly in a denied-area location, and then you never see them again, that was always very hard for me. I remember I recruited a good agent, I needed to turn him over, he met multiple people—analysts and other agents—and he said to me 'I'm really just doing this for you.'"

But not all of Marc's recruits were people he enjoyed developing a relationship with.

---

* A quick interaction between case officer and agent at a location where it would be hard to observe their quick encounter.

"I remember one time with a senior official from an Arab country that, because of his spotty human-rights record, I really didn't like—a true hardcore idealogue—and I was trying to find out what that true link would be to develop the relationship. I told him I was reading the Syrian philosopher Michel Aflaq's writing on the Arab world, and it turned out the guy was hugely influenced by Aflaq; and he was so impressed that I had read Aflaq that it caused him to trust me" and ultimately put Marc on the path of successfully handling this senior official, despite the blood on his hands.

As a salesperson, you won't necessarily have to play in such a gutter. If someone is truly sketchy, it probably makes good business sense to walk away. But I'm talking about the type of person who is just arrogant enough to make your life unpleasant, just dismissive enough of you and your role in trying to sell them that you'd prefer to walk away; but you have a job to do, just like the case officer recruiting a new agent.

Spies talk about practicing radical empathy as a path toward building rapport with someone it might not come naturally with. Maybe it's a terrorist they want to recruit to get inside his organization. This person has worked to support actions that have killed civilians for his organization's extremist aims—this is not an easy person to find something likable in.

But scratch below the surface and there is almost always something human and relatable. Even if a person has extremist religious ideas, they may also have a deep sense of family and demonstrate devotion and kindness to them. Maybe they are deeply mindful of tenets in their religion regarding charity and have shown a strong willingness to sacrifice for the less fortunate.

None of this excuses their awful flaws. But the spy must find a way to relate to this person, to genuinely connect with them, and so they compartmentalize (but don't ignore) their judgment about their target's terrible flaws and focus on what makes this person relatable in the recruitment process.

Surely you can do the same with someone with far less serious shortcomings.

The former spy who shared the quote about the bond between a case officer and agent now works in corporate America, and she often feels estranged from her sales team. She sees them engaged in deceptive practices, for instance telling prospective clients that an event her company is hosting has almost no spaces left when there are plenty of spots available. She knows that sooner or later the chickens will come home to roost; and while a salesperson might pull off a short-term win with those kinds of tactics, they won't build an enduring relationship. People are naturally skeptical of salespeople; and any hint that you're confirming their bias will likely end the relationship. Trust is hard to build and easy to lose.

So beneath her quote about a real bond existing between the case officer and her agent is the fact that it's about connection, not deception.

A former colleague provides an example from a sales perspective, one that is more focused on long-term relationships.

Bartley O'Dwyer is one of the most effective salespeople I've known, and he combines natural charisma with a deep understanding of financial services. He worked at one particular consulting firm for fifteen years and was highly successful there. But it wasn't only the deals he closed there that benefited his career; it was the relationships he fostered over those many years.

When he left for a new job and turned to his network to drum up business, he was surprised that many of the contacts that he had cultivated over time but had never managed to convert into clients were under the impression that they, in fact, had been clients of his in the past. Because of the continued outreach he had had with them, and because of the events and other gives he had provided, and because he had made that outreach not contingent on closing a particular deal but rather based on developing real relationships, he was able to get these contacts to consider working with him at his new job. Indeed, they actually thought they were simply continuing to do business with him, because he had been so steadfast in keeping up the relationship over many years. It has proven instrumental in the early success he's had in his new role.

Finding ways to connect with your sales targets, just as spies do with their intelligence targets, will help you build longer-term, more durable, and more fulfilling relationships with your clients. Those kinds of relationships can lead to all sorts of fruitful outcomes beyond making the initial sale. It might lead to a valuable referral to win another client; perhaps they will hire you for their own sales team. Maybe, like Bartley, those contacts cultivated over the years by engaging in relationship development and not being overly transactional will result in early wins in a new job. Taking an even wider perspective, building relationships built on true connections will lead to a richer, more satisfying life.

An important postscript to this thought is another spy maxim: *good spies re-recruit their agents at every meeting.* Don't take your client for granted once you've made the sale—the journey is just beginning.

One of the lessons on connection that I've learned is that *vulnerability breeds intimacy, and humanity builds credibility.* Sharing details about yourself, even your struggles, bridges a gap between you and your sales target. From John Sipher: "If you're expecting someone to open up and tell you things that they wouldn't tell anyone else, you have to share about your weaknesses and problems yourself."

An example from my personal life will make this clear.

In the summer of 2011 I was leaving one corporate security company to take a bigger opportunity with another—leading the business-intelligence practice at a fascinating boutique firm. I was planning a trip to the Caribbean to do some scuba-diving in the few weeks off I had built in before my start date.

I had noticed in recent months that the hearing in my right ear wasn't as good as it had been. In fact, when I had my headphones on, the hearing in my right ear was very muffled, a big problem for a music fanatic like me.

I journeyed into the medical wilderness and, after much poking and prodding, doctors determined that I had a somewhat rare but thankfully benign tumor called an acoustic neuroma. Little bigger than a quarter, and potentially growing in my head for a dozen years, it was choking off the auditory nerve in my right ear.

The scuba-diving trip went out the window as I worried about the Bell's palsy that could arise from leaving the tumor unchecked. I was told that the procedure to remove it would likely result in permanent hearing loss in my right ear, and that's exactly what happened. I'm thankful that being deaf in my right ear was the only long-term physical consequence that resulted from the long and complicated surgery to remove this tumor (and scuba-diving the only activity I can't engage in again as a result).

I say *physical consequence,* because the overall consequence to my life has been more significant, and an odd silver lining developed.

When I meet people in a crowded restaurant, I want to sit with as many people as possible to my left so I can hear the best I can. When I'm walking on the street I always walk to the person's right for the same reason, often dancing around them to get to walk with them on my good side. I often need to explain why I'm doing these things.

When I share even very briefly the reason for my left-sidedness, an extraordinary thing happens.

Walls come down and suddenly I am a human being to these people and not just a salesperson. This kind of epiphany from a target is especially evident when I'm in a business environment where everyone has their armor of professionalism up. When they hear about what I went through, these people instantly see me in different terms—not as someone who is trying to sell to them, not as someone they need to be wary of, but rather as someone who has endured something scary. There is a saying that not everyone experiences tragedy, but we've all experienced misfortune and can relate to that in others.

How do people often reply when I tell them about my hearing loss? They share something personal about what they or a loved one or close friend has been through. They respond to me *in kind*, an aspect of human behavior which we will get into further. Sharing what I've been through and getting my target to respond and see my humanity offers avenues for connection.

I don't mention my hearing loss to be a more effective salesperson; I mention it for tactical reasons—because I want to be able to hear better, so I take steps to put myself in a position to do so. But I have learned not to be shy about mentioning it, because I like connecting with people; and by humanizing myself in this way, I find I can break down barriers.

Spies know this secret and use it when they can. One former case officer—a longtime CIA veteran who was station chief in important foreign capitals—who I'll call Tom,* told me about relating to his agents through family ties. He has a child on the autism spectrum, and sharing this with prospective agents who wanted to talk about family allowed him to bond with them.

Another case officer shares a story about a secret his agent shared that made him feel like an outcast in his society and vulnerable because of what he believed—or, rather, didn't believe.

This potential agent, a diplomat from a deeply religious Islamic nation, was being cultivated by a case officer in a Western country that they were both stationed in. A playful relationship had developed between the case officer and this diplomat, one in which they teased each other about their respective countries and tested each other's beliefs.

At dinner one night, this case officer said he was going to order some pork and a beer, and he gave this diplomat a wink. The diplomat sighed and said, "You know, things aren't always what they seem," and ordered the same thing.

The diplomat then confessed to his new friend that he didn't believe in Islam, or even God, and he had been faking it all his life. There was no one in his life he could share this with; indeed, he had never told anyone this secret, which could certainly cost him his job and could actually endanger the welfare of his family. But he had a hunger to share this with someone and to debate the existence of God and the good of religion.

This case officer made this diplomat feel comfortable, made him feel like his secret was safe with him. He also made him feel like he was someone he could have theological discussions with because the case officer, perhaps sensing a secular orientation inside this diplomat, had been testing him at the edges about his religion. The confession by the diplomat made him vulnerable, and they drew closer together, with the case officer soon able to make his confession (*I'm a case officer.*) to the atheistic diplomat and turn him into an agent.

Exactly how to share vulnerabilities is a deeply personal choice. You might not be comfortable sharing something as personal as what Tom and I share regularly with those that we are seeking to connect with. But I hope you will think about our stories, the idea of sharing more of yourself, and put yourself out there. You will distinguish your humanity, which will work *with* and not against your job. And it's a good practice in not only work, but also in daily life.

Think of the Covid pandemic era. I found a silver lining during the worst of it. While we were all getting burned out on our video meetings, I found it refreshing to see clients in their homes, to observe their kitchens, living rooms, and bedrooms; to have them Zoom-bombed by their kids, spouses, or pets; to be wearing T-shirts and sweatpants instead of business suits. I found that while I missed the in-person interaction—and nothing could replace that—the oddness of virtually being in a client's home, while we were all stuck living through a truly scary pandemic, created an intimacy that was refreshing and helped us all to let our guards down a bit and to see the humanity in all of us behind our carefully constructed professional facades.

## KARAOKE WITH THE STRONGMAN

Greg Roberts has a unique profile when it comes to connectivity and relating it to sales. Having left active duty, Greg's LinkedIn profile lists that he "more than doubled business development activities" in one of his postings with the Agency. Those sales targets were new agents recruited to collect intelligence, and Greg notes that the way agent recruitment was talked about within the Agency wasn't that different from sales-world usage of terms like "funnel" and "pipeline."

But Greg's unique understanding of selling like a spy was not only sourced from his time as a CIA case officer, but also from earlier in his career when he spent years in the military with the Green Berets.

Among the special-forces community, no other team is as revered for their powers of connectivity as the Green Berets. Though not as celebrated as the SEALs or Delta Force, the Green Berets are famous for their ability to work with whatever they have so they can achieve their mission. Also unlike the SEALs or Delta Force, at least in recent years, the Green Berets are less like commandos kicking down doors and more like the group that drops in behind enemy lines and recruits indigenous forces to collaborate. According to Greg, "The thing that Green Berets really master is being able to use everything in their reach to help us move our objective forward. Whatever resource we have, we'll figure out how to apply it to the problem at hand, whether it's been used for that before or not. We're always in an under-resourced environment— our whole method of operation is about being just dropped into a country and isolated after that, so you need to use anything at your disposal to succeed in the mission."

As a salesperson, application of this mindset is an asset. Let's say you're at a conference. You've been resourced with your sharp business outfit, training in the sector you're selling to, and an expense account to entertain clients. But at that moment, you're behind enemy lines and need to use your wits to succeed. This means being able to adjust to the culture around you (for instance, the pace and ethos of Las Vegas) and the personalities you're dealing with.

It's one thing for a case officer to overcome the considerable cultural challenges of relationship-building with someone from India or Angola. But the challenges Green Berets face when it comes to connectivity can be even greater when you consider that they have been tasked with connecting with isolated cultures like the Hmong in Southeast Asia, little changed over hundreds of years.

One of Greg's most important lessons was that you can't be "obsequious or milquetoast; you can't do the job and be a squish. That's ultimately why indigenous cultures follow us—we have a moral compass; it makes us more authentic to them. If you're going to have a relationship with them, you need to be someone they can respect. Nobody likes a squish; nobody is going to give any-thing to someone they don't respect. That means being authentic and knowing who you are, and you approach it with a clear mind. Having things you stand for or won't abide and being clear about it is important for building rapport with someone. The flip side is that you can't be judgmental."

At times in Greg's career of connectivity under difficult circumstances, he played with different personas, but he consistently returned to the lesson of being authentic as the best way to connect with someone. "I thought it could be good to not have any hard edges, just to go along with whatever someone liked and was into, to get to know them better. But people are good at sussing out what's authentic and what's not."

Salespeople learn that same lesson over time—how to walk the line of being respectful and interested in who someone is, but also maintaining your own backbone, your own sense of self and what your values are. Ultimately, clients—whether they are indigenous people in far-flung parts of the world or a corporate executive considering a vendor—want to spend time with someone they can respect, not someone who seems to have no true character—a "squish," as Greg puts it.

One of Greg's most memorable assignments was a counter-terrorism mission in Asia. He can't share too many details, so the account you see here includes the actual edits and redactions made by the CIA for this book.

We knew that ███████████████████████ this area was host to an array of terrorist groups, the most notorious of which ███████████████ were aligned with Al Qaeda. This group took locals and Westerners hostage and killed quite a few of them. They presented a serious challenge to the stability of ████████████████████████ ██████████████████████████ ████████ this area.

Greg's team had intelligence on a few terrorists, but they needed to operate in an area controlled by

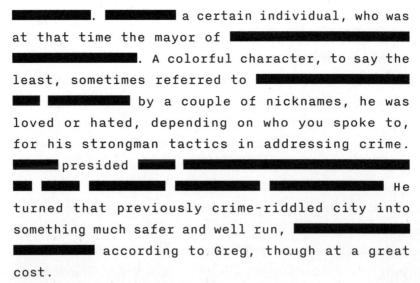

██████████. ██████████ a certain individual, who was at that time the mayor of ████████████████████ ██████████████████. A colorful character, to say the least, sometimes referred to ██████████████████ ████ ██████████████ by a couple of nicknames, he was loved or hated, depending on who you spoke to, for his strongman tactics in addressing crime. ███████presided █████ ████████████████████████ ███ ██████ ██████████ ██████████ ██████████████ He turned that previously crime-riddled city into something much safer and well run, ████████████ ████████████ according to Greg, though at a great cost.

One of the tactics Greg acquired in his career in the CIA and Green Berets was to always look to recruit an "explainer." Navigating the many exotic cultures Greg needed to work in required humility—understanding that you don't know every-thing is the first step toward opening yourself up to wisdom. Greg learned to seek out someone who could help him understand the environment he was operating in, and that started with a macro-assessment of the culture, then a more nuanced approach to the organization he was looking to penetrate or operate with or against, and down to the more granular level of the people or partic-ular person he needed to influence.

When it came to █████████████, the strongman, Greg had his man—a foul-mouthed ████████████ who enjoyed shocking others with his violent stories. He helped Greg understand the distinct and somewhat volatile persona of ████████████████ the strongman.

████████████████████████████████████ He had
already cozied up to the Chinese, ████ ████████
████████████████████████████████. He was skeptical of the Americans, surely with the Chinese
whispering in his ear. He liked to drink and
carouse and would be suspicious, the explainer
noted, if the Americans wouldn't participate in
his nighttime activities. But Greg knew that he
needed to maintain his professionalism and not
go too far in following ████████ him down his
debauched rabbit hole. The explainer noted that
████████ he operated by instinct and Greg and his
colleagues would need to walk a fine line between
masking any disapproval of ████████ his partying
while maintaining their professionalism.

They met ████████ the strongman, who had already
been drinking, at a favorite karaoke bar. It was a
surreal scene: a drunken strongman singing off-key
under disorienting lights with sycophants flutter-
ing around him. Greg fell back on one of the rules
of special forces: "Always look cool. Always know
where you're at and if you don't know where you're
at, look cool. Having that persona that you're not
flustered helps, it shows to others it's not gonna
be a disaster. It helps build trust. We needed to
show that we were there to do a counterterrorism
operation. We wanted to show that we were serious
and that meant how you presented yourself — your
dress, posture, tone of voice. All of it needs to
be under control, put together. It was about having
a firm handshake with ████████ him. I wanted to
present myself as serious but informal, smile and

joke a bit, show I was not a robot, but maintain professionalism, all of which was based on the coaching I got from my explainer."

Greg and the team walked that fine line all night, not drinking too much and not taking a turn on the karaoke mic ("that was for ████████ him"). The ████████ strongman ultimately agreed to the operation in his backyard. Greg points to the lessons he was trained in throughout his clandestine career, as well as the essential input of his explainer, in analyzing his success that night. He says the same lessons can be applied successfully in the corporate world as well.

As for the mission, Greg, the tight-lipped laconic Midwestern spy that he is, will only note that it happened and was successful. It doesn't seem that those terrorists operated in ████████ the strongman's wild kingdom for much longer after that strange evening.

## KEY TAKEAWAYS

Spies utilize an elite set of skills when it comes to connecting with a vast array of humanity, and there are many compelling lessons we can take from the world of espionage when it comes to connecting with people in our careers and everyday lives. Salesmanship is at the heart of spy tradecraft and how they make their most difficult of sales. Using the same methods to overcome difficult people and forge connections, you can differentiate yourself in a crowded marketplace.

1. Spies are a misunderstood group. Far from the world of James Bond, they are elite relationship managers who often resemble talented account executives or psychiatrists, rather than Jason Bourne types.

2. We can't hit it off with everyone, so practice *radical empathy* when it comes to trying to influence someone you're not connecting with easily. Spies know that each of us has a kernel of humanity, and they focus on that aspect of their targets, not the many negatives.

3. Make yourself vulnerable to connect more deeply to your targets. This move can be a particularly good strategy to change the tone of an encounter with a target that is not responsive to your rapport-building efforts. Utilize our inherent tendency to respond to things in kind to get your target to open up as well.

4. Your own interests are essential when it comes to connecting, but you should cultivate intellectual curiosity to get to know your targets and show that you respect who they are.

5. Cultures can vary widely even within the same country, so be mindful of the particularities of where your targets are located and the groups they are part of. Do your best to adhere to local cultures and demonstrate a respect for their traditions, but don't lose sight of your own identity.

# 2

# THE ART OF **CONVERSATION**

*How to listen better, get answers
without asking questions, and connect quicker*

We were on our way to a meeting, but we couldn't find the office that was our destination. My colleague was a former intelligence officer, a WASPy charmer with an easy laugh and friendly persona that hid an astute and calculating intellect. The combination had made her a successful case officer during her time in Central/Eastern Europe, where she worked for the Agency on nuclear proliferation issues.

I pulled out my phone for the map application to get a better sense of where our client's office was. My colleague casually asked just to see the map and shared an offhand remark that has stayed with me ever since.

"Because of my training, I can typically have a fast look at a map and quickly figure out where I am and where I need to go." And that's exactly what she did. She quickly led us right to our client's office.

Map-reading had never been my strong suit, yet I found the skill to be fascinating.

Now, it wasn't something my colleague had been born with. When the CIA tested her in the recruitment process, it revealed strong analytical skills, but she was then *trained* in map-reading, and she practiced it extensively to refine it to a point that it was second nature.

I want to stress how important and valuable it is to practice these skills in your everyday life. By doing that with the skills and concepts in this book, you will become better and better at them until they become natural parts of your tool kit when it comes to connecting with people and learning about them, just like my colleague who had practiced her map-reading skills over and over again until they were essentially a reflex.

Practicing these skills in everyday life will also build stronger relationships in your personal life. You'll find that you are better understood by friends and family while also having a better understanding of them. And it will increase your social currency as someone who is an excellent conversationalist.

The skills I'm going to share with you—sourced directly from my observations and experiences working with case officers and other highly trained former government officials—are all skills that we, everyday people, can utilize and benefit from if we practice them. They will improve your relationships—and, on the professional side, help you to grow into a more effective salesperson.

## ELICITATION

A former case officer shared a story about a CIA training exercise when I prodded him about conversation skills and developing knowledge of a potential target.

The trainers at The Farm took a cohort of aspiring case officers to a little seaside town and gave them a simple mission: spot a target, approach them, and learn as much as you can without asking any direct questions.

You might be asking yourself "How do you learn about someone without asking any direct questions?"

Well, let's say this spy-class exercise takes place in the middle of May and it is an unseasonably hot day. You spot your target, walk up to him, and start making small talk. Perhaps you say something like "Wow, what a scorcher! I grew up in the Pacific Northwest and it doesn't get this hot even at the height of summer. Man, I'm really melting today."

Nothing else is said; the statement is just left dangling there.

Perhaps the target replies "Oh, well, I'm originally from South Florida and it's this hot or hotter for most of the year, so I'm used to this kind of heat."

No question was asked, but now our budding spy knows a little something about their target. A modest start, but something to build on nonetheless.

This is the skill of elicitation.

Elicitation is defined as "the act of drawing out or bringing forth emotions, opinions, facts, etc." Elicitation often involves asking questions, but they are frequently questions that mask the true interest of the questioner. It is a more strategic way to collect information.

Elicitation is a useful skill for a spy and a sales professional alike.

Spy or salesperson, when you meet a potential target you want to learn as much as you can about the target. But asking a bunch of questions, especially very direct ones, can make someone feel like they're being interrogated. What might have started as a nice get-to-know-you encounter leads to defensiveness or skepticism—not what the spy or salesperson wants.

Elicitation offers a chance to get to know people and secure valuable information, in a more circumspect manner. Let's talk about some examples from everyday life, the spy world, and the sales world.

*The Surprise Party*

Let's say you are throwing your friend Sara a surprise party, and you want to know what Sara's favorite food is so you can have it on hand for the big party. None of Sara's friends are any help. Nobody remembers what her favorite food is.

But you have an idea.

You give Sara a call and suggest making a dinner plan for next week. "Sara, I heard about this great Thai restaurant in my neighborhood—didn't you tell me once that Thai is your favorite food?"

Sara replies, "Sure, let's do Thai next week, but I'm not sure where you got Thai being my favorite food! Pizza is actually my favorite food."

Now you know what food to have at Sara's party to make it as fun and enjoyable as possible for her, and you didn't have to ask her a specific question that might have led to suspicion and ruining the surprise. If you had said "Sara, remind me: What's your favorite food again?" you might have spoiled the whole plan. Sara could start thinking, *Hmm, that's a strange question to ask out of the blue. My birthday is coming up in a few weeks, maybe my friends are planning something....*

Instead, you asked a question that you either knew to be false or had no reason to believe was true—a question you expected Sara would have been likely to correct.

That is one of the cornerstones of elicitation. Behavioral science has demonstrated that human beings have a *tendency to correct,* especially when it comes to details about themselves. We're all the heroes of our own stories, and we take particular care to make sure the record is set straight when it comes to details about ourselves.

It would have been strange for Sara to say "Thai isn't my favorite, but it's fine for dinner tomorrow night." No, she wants to set the record straight: pizza is actually her favorite food.

*The Mining Consultant*
You're a case officer in Jakarta, Indonesia, and you're at a business conference at a fancy hotel. You meet a mining consultant who you think might be an interesting target, and you're trying to figure out what might motivate this person to cooperate and become your agent.

You engage in conversation, and then—

"Those are some fascinating points about the Indonesian mining industry," you might say as they wrap up some point about their work. "There are people that would pay a lot of money to hear those kinds of insights on a regular basis." Again, you just leave it there, no question asked.

The target might respond in a couple of ways.

Perhaps they light up and say "Really? Wow, I'd love to earn some extra money." If they say this, you know that financial incentives might be the ticket to recruitment.

If they just shrug their shoulders and seem uninterested in that comment, perhaps noting that they are already well-compensated, then you know that money is not the likely pathway to turning this person into an agent.

But you didn't ask any probing question that would make the target uncomfortable or reveal your true intention. You made a statement that obscured your true intention and helped you figure out what your next step might be, with your target leading the way.

A quick digression from our examples of elicitation:

What we saw in the mining-consultant example was a case officer assessing what might motivate someone to say yes to their very particular sales offer. This is a vital part of agent development, and motivation is not thought about enough in the sales world when it comes to client development.

There are typically a select number of motivations for a foreign national to spy for the U.S. government. Money, as we saw with the mining consultant, is one of the most common motivations. Sometimes it involves children—perhaps someone wants to get their child the superior educational opportunities that are available in the U.S., or it could be healthcare for a sick child that is unavailable in their home country but provided at the highest level in America. It could be because a diplomat is from an ethnic group that has faced persecution, and they are aggrieved. Patriotism, strangely enough, can encourage someone to betray their country if they believe their country is on the wrong track. And finally, sometimes plain old ego or a lust for adventure can be that espionage trigger.

Case officers, along with their support team of analysts, spend a lot of time considering what might motivate someone and leverage all sorts of resources to determine what might be a useful course of action to develop that particular foreign national.

In the corporate world, most salespeople think "I have a great product/service, I'm a charming person, they should want to buy from me once they hear our value proposition and are wowed by my amazing personality." That certainly often works, but understanding motivation can unlock a more productive and/or efficient avenue to make the sale.

Perhaps you're visiting a prospect and have learned that there was recently a power struggle on the team. The previous manager is now out, and there is a new one in place. She has agreed to take a meeting with you after the previous manager had spurned your outreach for a while. You should be thinking about how, because she wants to put a new stamp on her regime, she is now considering all the vendors who work with her team. Your pitch should subtly allude to this new dynamic, without going too far, which might let her see what you're doing.

That's just one example. Would your pitch be strengthened by understanding someone's ambition and positioning yourself and what you're selling as a way to make them look good? Is there a particular dynamic—say, delivery time—that you've assessed as the main pain point for a client?

Think like a spy when assessing what might motivate a potential client to work with you, and use elicitation to draw out those dynamics to help you chart a successful path forward.

*Sales Sleuthing*

You're an account executive. A client has an annual retainer for services with your consulting firm, and it's coming up for renewal in under two months. The metrics for servicing this client are flat year-over-year: not much about their usage is trending in a way that gives you a sense of whether the client might be primed for an upsell, or whether you risk a downgrade or even cancellation of your service. You're operating without enough information to formulate a good plan to renew their retainer.

So you decide on a gambit to see if you can elicit some information to help you plan for the renewal discussion.

You call your client, Frank, and you say "Hey, Frank, I just wanted to give you a call because I heard a rumor that I found a little disturbing and wanted to see if there was any truth to it. I heard with Q2 ending, your company has had two consecutive rough quarters and I'm hearing whispers about budget cuts and layoffs. I just wanted to reach out and see if there was anything I can do to be helpful."

Frank might reply and say "Well, I think you have it backwards, actually. Both quarters have gone really well, and my team in particular is thriving; we'll likely have a bigger budget next year, and I'm planning on doing some hiring in Q4. You better get some new sources!"

Now you have much more information to plan your renewal because, just as with Sara and eliciting her favorite food, you posed a couple of questions that you either knew to be false or just didn't know were based on the truth and gambled that the *tendency to correct* would assist you in getting the information you needed.

It surely did in this case, but it was also aided by another behavioral tendency: *professional pride*. Not only did Frank want to correct the record, but he also had professional pride, which reinforced the tendency to correct. Frank is proud of the fact that his company has done well so far this year, that his team is growing under his leadership, and he doesn't want a professional acquaintance of his thinking anything otherwise. He wanted to do just a bit of bragging because of his professional pride, bragging that provides you with helpful information.

But if you're making that call to Frank, you don't want to just jump into rumors about budget cuts and layoffs and then ask if there's anything you can do to help. If you did so, Frank might get off the phone with you and think *That question was pretty odd; it was the opposite of what was going on. I wonder if there was something else behind his call. . . .*

Obviously, we don't want our targets wondering such things about our intentions. So spies use the **violin conversation** to help mask these attempts at elicitation.

The violin conversation is based on the fact that people tend to remember the beginning and end of conversations much more than the middle of them. Violins are skinny at the end and their substance is in the middle. When played right, the violin can make beautiful music and if you use the violin conversation, you'll play your target like an instrument and make your own beautiful conversational music.

So to use the violin conversation, you're better off calling Frank and making some small talk, asking him about a project you just completed for his team, *then* make your attempt at elicitation, and finish up with some plans about an upcoming project and a little more small talk before wrapping up the conversation. The elicitation attempt sandwiched right in the middle is far less likely to draw the kind of scrutiny you want to avoid.

Violin conversations are useful beyond just elicitation. A salesperson who attended a talk of mine reached out to share an interesting application. Sam* was taking an important client to lunch, chasing a potential new deal worth more than $100k. Meanwhile, Sam's accounting team was after him to collect on the same client's unpaid bill of just under $10k Eager to placate his accounting team but worried about the awkward dynamics of bringing up the unpaid bill, Sam used the violin conversation. He brought up the unpaid bill briefly in the middle of the conversation over lunch, and his client agreed to get the bill sorted. Sam had only to briefly bring up the unpleasant business of the unpaid bill, knowing his client was unlikely to linger on the issue. The other side of the violin conversation gave him the opportunity to close the new, lucrative deal.

Another big prompt for elicitation is one that is fairly universal—gossip. Counter-intelligence officers will tell you that it's often the case that the person leaking sensitive information is not one of the key decision-makers but rather one of the associates, assistants, and administrators that hover around such decision-makers. The underlings want to feel important, part of the action, and will frequently be the ones who are doing the leaking.

I keep that in mind when I meet people who are from a target organization I'm interested in. Someone might not be part of the specific team I'm targeting or might not have the right role to influence my sale, but that person might know the people I need to influence. That person might potentially share insights with me, some rumors or details about the company or its culture. All this can be helpful if you keep an open mind and big-picture focus.

Because of people's tendency to gossip, I tend to cultivate the executive assistant whenever I can. In addition to being key to getting my phone calls and emails returned and getting on the calendar of the decision-maker, the executive assistant is at the crossroads of important stuff happening at any organization. Getting in good with that person, treating them with respect and cultivating them, has led to my collection of important insights that have helped me on numerous occasions.

Flattery is another good way to elicit important details. Usually when someone is overtly flattered, they tend to self-deprecate and explain the source of their success more than they would if they were directly asked about something.

Asking for help can get people to open up, too. Most of us want to be kind; so if you ask someone for their knowledge or insight as a way to assist you with something, they will often say more than if they are asked directly.

There are many other reasons why people share information, often sensitive information, if you're ready to be strategic about getting it.

Adam* was a military interrogator before joining the corporate world. In his new role, he'd use some of the elicitation skills he cultivated in government service.

For a client seeking information on an organization, Adam would plant himself at a local bar near the factory of said company. He would dress like a blue-collar local, order a draft beer around the time the factory was letting out for the day, and chat up the workers who would sit next to him. He would start with a basic question about how their shift had been, before moving the conversation to how much volume the factory was doing, whether the guys were doing a lot of overtime, how the union relationship with the factory was, and so forth. Ultimately, he would leave with information that no investor listening to an earnings call would learn, valuable insights that could help an investor make decisions about whether to buy or sell a stock.

Tom, the former station chief we met earlier, shared how he used asking for help to "get someone into the routine of sharing information with me." I call it *the stumbling ask*.

He would say something like "Hey, I'm working on a project, and I was wondering if I could ask for your help on something. . . ." Then he would pause, break eye contact, and say "You know what, it's probably best if I don't put you out, I don't want you to feel that our relationship is about a quid pro quo. . . ." What he would usually find is that that person would then insist on learning more about the project and want to help. In these cases, the request to help, and to provide information, feels to the target like it was their idea, not you asking for a favor.

To understand how well this works, think about someone telling you that they want to ask you something, but then they backtrack by saying "Oh, maybe I shouldn't ask about that." You get curious and want to know what this person is talking about, right? And once you've pushed to learn what they are thinking about ("No, it's okay. Ask me anything."), you then look at the request differently because you insisted on learning what it was.

Tom used the sentence "I don't want our relationship to seem like it's a quid pro quo." It reinforces that he is really seeking a deeper *relationship* with that person, not something more transactional. It helps set the stage for cultivation. The person on the receiving end of the stumbling question would then follow up at later meetings, asking about how the project was going, feeling like a participant, and they would subtly move along on the process of becoming an agent. The parallels with cultivating a contact in the business world are quite clear.

You should also cultivate awkward silences to elicit information. People hate awkward silences and will often blurt things out, sometimes very interesting things, in order to break the spell of silence. So get comfortable with awkward pauses in conversation.

A key to all these methods is to make them your own. Practice these techniques with your friends and family, with whom sloppy mistakes aren't particularly costly. Try a variety of approaches, matching them ideally to your own personal style of conversation and interaction.

The art of eliciting information is at the center of spy tradecraft, and has been since the world's second-oldest profession has been around. One compelling historical practitioner of the art is the famous Israeli spy Eli Cohen.

Born in 1924 in the cosmopolitan stew of Alexandria, Egypt, Eli spoke five languages and was a gifted clandestine agent whom many people credit with contributing to both the brevity and the victory of Israel against its neighbors in the Six-Day War of 1967.

Eli immigrated to Israel after state-sponsored attacks on the Jewish community in Egypt made life untenable. Deeply familiar with Arab culture, he became an invaluable spy for the nascent Jewish state against the many enemies scheming against it.

In an audacious plot, he infiltrated high society in Damascus in the early 1960s, despite Syria's being a police state and highly dangerous for any Jew. Israel knew that Syria was plotting new ways to attack, but it had no visibility into these strategies until Eli Cohen made his way up the upper rungs of Syria's capital city.

Once there, you could say Eli's job was solely to elicit the intentions and plans of the Syrians and share them with his spy handlers.

The Netflix miniseries *The Spy* starring Sacha Baron Cohen does a great job showing the subtlety of spy tradecraft. Early in the series, Eli has cultivated the military leader and future dictator Hafez al-Assad. Eli is trying to get the proper documents to enter the paranoid state of Syria, and when visiting Hafez he uses something similar to "the stumbling ask," mentioning that he has secured a recommendation letter for his entrance, which he "hopes will be sufficient." Hafez takes the bait and says "Oh, please, I will write you another one." Eli (posing as Kamel Amin Thaabet) replies "Oh, no, that's too much to ask," and Hafez scoffs at Eli's modesty, saying "Nonsense, it would be my privilege." Eli had elicited what he needed from Hafez and furthermore made it feel like it was Hafez's idea.

Later on in the series, Eli needs to learn what Mohamed bin-Laden (Osama bin-Laden's father) is doing in Syria, meeting with Assad. He presses the new information minister, who he has cultivated, for information, but the minister is wary. Eli uses the trigger of the minister's professional pride, wondering what good an information minister is if he doesn't have good information. The minister won't reveal the reason, only noting that he's happy to share secrets with Kamal. However, "the ones that might get you murdered are the ones I'm discreet about," the minister says. Kamal doesn't learn the exact reason for the influential Saudi's presence in Syria, but he elicits enough to know that it is far from a benign visit and that there is indeed something for the Israelis to be alarmed about.

In a scene soon afterward, he encourages gossip to garner further intelligence. In talking with the same minister, as well as the son of Hafez al-Assad (Bashar al-Assad, the modern-day Syrian dictator), he learns that a top general in the previous regime has attempted suicide because of the torture he was undergoing.

Throughout the series, Kamal puts himself in the best position to elicit information by pushing the right human buttons to trigger the responses that he needs. While Eli was eventually caught and executed by the Syrians, the information he secured through elicitation played an essential role in safeguarding the Israeli state as its enemies plotted against it.

At the heart of all these elicitation ideas is that people are naturally eager to share. That is why elicitation works.

I was once on a panel at a prestigious graduate school speaking about corporate investigations when a student asked, "Why do people agree to answer your questions?"

A great question in and of itself, and it gets to an essential human trait that I have observed as a journalist, as a corporate investigator, and as a salesman: people like being asked their opinion. As a case officer put it to me, "People want to tell their story."

We have a natural tendency to want to share our points of view. Even when I was reporting from a place like China—where you would think people would be afraid or reluctant to talk to a Western journalist—eagerness to share was the case. Aside from certain sensitive topics, the Chinese were, like everyone I've encountered, flattered to be asked their opinion and willing to tell me what they thought. Another key component of elicitation is the ability to be a great active listener, the most important—and most challenging—of the spy skills that will help you to succeed. Let's listen in.

## ACTIVE LISTENING

Let's face it: most people in a conversation aren't *really* listening. They're just waiting for their turn to speak when in a conversation. We listen with the intention to reply, not the intention to understand. We hear what the other person is saying, and suddenly mental sparks fly—*oh, I have an even better anecdote I can tell!* Or *I want to share my opinion on this subject!* Of course, we are doing *some* degree of listening to what our conversational counterpart is saying, but we are often listening on a superficial level, gathering key words in our brain to get the gist and then searching our mental database for our view on what we're hearing. Because we all engage in this waiting-for-our-turn-to-speak, there is an opportunity for the truly dedicated listener to distinguish themselves.

Talk to spies, FBI agents, and others in law enforcement, and you will hear over and over again just how important active listening is. Carl* notes: "The willingness to stop talking, and really listen, and let people tell you their story" is a huge part of the job of any case officer. "Everybody thinks they're the most important person, the most interesting person, and they want to tell their story. And they want to tell that story to a diplomat or someone with high status: that gives value to them, helps with their self-image." That comment brought me back to my time as a young journalist flattered to be asked by a diplomat about what I was hearing from editors.

Marc Polymeropoulos notes the importance of a spy's being a good listener: "The greatest skill you can have is to listen and not talk. If you're always talking as an intelligence officer, you're going to miss things. If I handle an agent for a few years, oftentimes the only outlet they have is with me, their case officer, they have compartmentalized their life so much. You're their shrink; they're telling you things they wouldn't tell their spouses."

The good news is that while listening is the most important spy skill there is, you don't need to be trained at The Farm to be a good listener. The bad news is that it is very hard to actually *be* a good listener.

"I'm chatty and outgoing," Marc notes about the difficulty of active listening. "I have to battle all my natural impulses, tell myself to shut up; my job is only to listen, not impress you. At the end of the day, I have to walk away from this short meeting in an Iraqi alley with information. Sometimes these operational encounters are super-brief, so I had to make decisions on the fly and had to be listening carefully."

Active listening is often the Achilles' heel of even the most talented salespeople. I'm thinking of a couple I've known over the years, charismatic, intelligent, and empathetic individuals who draw people to them through their winning personalities. They are deeply knowledgeable about the industry they work in and passionate about the value the services they're selling can bring to their clients.

But go on a pitch with them, and they start talking and often go on and on, indulging in long soliloquies where the client or prospect doesn't get a chance to speak for quite a while. I always cringed when this happened during meetings I attended with these highly successful salespeople.

Adam,* the military interrogator who has gone into the business world, notes that "Being an interrogator tunes you in to whether your target is receiving the message you're trying to deliver. There's what you say, there's the meaning you intend, and then there is the meaning that the receiver interprets. In sales there is a lot I want to say, a meaning I want to create with you; but if there is a dissonance, you're going to miss that meaning." That dissonance is often the result of salespeople falling in love with their own voice.

Speaking with sales teams, I urge them to practice their "elevator pitch"—the distilled version of their value proposition that you should be able to share in a brief elevator ride—until it is highly refined. Write it out and be brutal in culling every word until each one left is absolutely vital in describing what you do and why it is special.

I train them to practice their broader pitch in a way that breaks it up into segments punctuated by clarification questions that provide breaks in their description, offering the client or prospect a chance to weigh in and participate in the conversation.

Adam* talks about the value of "an engaged push–pull response" with the client. As an example, if he was meeting with a client in Kansas City, he would have looked around at restaurants near their office and mentioned a couple he was thinking of trying. He would consciously say the name of one or two wrong, which would get the client or prospect to correct him. It is a small thing, but it produces that back-and-forth in conversation and "creates commonality of experience, elicits a response, and it makes them actively listen and be engaged with what I'm saying. Now that we're talking about these restaurants, we have a shared experience." If there is a follow-up meeting or conversation, the topic of those restaurants can be returned to, the shared experience built upon.

Expand upon this method when you're talking about your product or service by breaking up your pitch with a clarification question. After you've been describing how your software can help streamline the procurement process, for example, asking "Do you have trouble managing multiple vendors and delivery schedules?" will give the prospect a chance to respond to what you've been saying, offer their thoughts on where your software might fit in to what they're doing, and create that "engaged pushback response" you're seeking.

The bottom line is that active listening, when done well, isn't about just shutting up: it's about creating a dynamic in conversation where both sides are listening carefully and learning from each other. You want the client to be learning from you about how great your product or service is, right? Then get off your pedestal, break up your pitch, and create engagement in client conversations that spurs mutual active listening.

There is no quick fix to becoming a great active listener, no trick that can be taught to suddenly make you get past what are significant natural hurdles. But if you can cultivate an active listening practice, over time you will improve. You might even get a reputation as a great conversationalist! Yes, people who have simply just been good active listeners are described that way.

The difficulties in active listening can be explained by psychology and behavioral science. Being mindful of these aspects of human behavior can help us get beyond each of our personal shortcomings in this area (because there is, of course, a variance in how well all of us listen—or, rather, don't listen). Understanding why active listening is so hard provides an opportunity to try to overcome those challenges.

One of the first facts is that "the human mind works four times faster than our verbal comprehension," notes Stephen Romano, a former chief hostage negotiator for the FBI. It's easy to see this. You're talking with someone, sharing an anecdote or opinion of yours, and you see their micro-expressions change—their eyes widen, their physical bearing shifts, and they can't wait for you to stop talking so they can tell you what they think. That's because they know where you're going with what you're saying, and you haven't even finished it yet. Again, you can see it in your conversational counterpart—they are nodding along, sometimes even finishing your sentence for you.

Opinions vary on the exact numbers, but Steve Romano believes (and studies have suggested) that our comprehension of a conversation is often actually based less than ten percent on the words spoken: everything else is about body language and tone of voice. While shocking, most behavioral psychologists will agree that our comprehension works in this way; but due to the variability of our personalities, that percentage will vary widely with people. The overall point still stands, nonetheless, and it's quite surprising—our listening tends to be more encompassing than we realize, picking up clues we're not consciously aware of, but less focused than we would think on the actual words we're hearing.

Renowned behavioral psychologist Dr. Mike Webster notes "Most of the time, we listen on a superficial level to hear certain words, or just long enough to get the gist of what someone is saying. Once we think we know where they're heading, our attention shifts back inward, where we silently compare what we heard to our own logic and worldview. Although we're still hearing the words that are being spoken (and may even nod in encouragement), we're mentally light-years away."

Perhaps you're like me, consistently frustrated by learning names. You meet someone and get their name, and it goes in one ear and right out the other. That's because when you meet someone, so much of your brain is devoted to assessing this person physically and measuring all the other intangibles, and we don't prioritize the name itself. We look at this new person we are meeting, and suddenly we are cavemen on the savannah: Is this a friend or foe? Is this a potential love interest? Et cetera. The name is not important to our atavistic brains at this moment.

One of the best first steps toward becoming an elite active listener is to address this name issue. Former FBI agent and legendary body language and behavior expert Joe Navarro tries to give the person another association other than their name, to help him remember someone. So if you meet a man who has his shirt unbuttoned a bit too much, showing his chest hair, and he tells you his name is Steve, you might have a better chance of remembering him as "chest-hair Steve." Joe will often write down someone's name or use the voice memo feature of his phone to quickly note someone's name and details about that person to help him remember them specifically.

Joe and I still often fail at remembering names despite these strategies, and he points out that "humans don't expect perfection. What humans expect is psychological comfort. Whoever provides that is going to be the winner. They don't expect you to remember their name, but for someone to say something like 'please forgive me: I've already forgotten your name, but I want to remember it.'" I will confess to forgetting someone's name and often striking a self-deprecating note about my memory when asking for their name again. And I will reshare my own name because quite often I believe they have not captured it either.

But once you have someone's name committed to memory, use it in conversation. We're all the stars of our own little universes, and there is no sweeter sound than hearing our name used. Using it subtly in conversation signals to your counterpart that you're focused on them, that they have your full attention, and that you respect them.


I have found it helpful to use a few analogies to illustrate conversational challenges. If you're a sports person, think about the actual words a sports broadcaster uses as the play-by-play account. The rest—what kind of season the batter is having, how the pitcher is having a career year ahead of free agency, and the fielding team's proclivity for errors—is the game's color commentary. The play-by-play is at the heart of things—just like the words are in a conversation—but the commentary is more closely followed. If you're more of a music person, think about a song's lyrics. They are like the words spoken in conversation. The melody encapsulates the whole song. We've all heard people misquote or misinterpret the lyrics of a song, and again we're back to the smaller role they play when it comes to assessing the song overall. We've all experienced humming along to a song and getting its emotional message, even if we don't know all the lyrics, right?

So, here are a few other suggestions for color commentary and melody to start you on the path to cultivating your active listening practice.

Make strong eye contact, but only for three or four seconds at a time so you don't freak out your counterpart. It will powerfully signal to them that you're with them, focused on them. Yes, it can be a challenge, especially when you're in a bustling restaurant or at a busy conference. Marc notes that "there is nothing worse than talking to someone you're trying to connect with, and their eyes are darting around, looking around for who else is there. What I practice and have trained young case officers to do is to lock in on that individual. You make that person feel like the most important person in the room." Combine that with using their name and asking encouraging questions geared toward learning more from them rather than passively waiting for them to finish so you can speak.

Quiet your body. Excessive fidgeting signals impatience, which should obviously be avoided. We'll get to much more about body language in a later chapter, but keep these details in mind and you'll be off to a good start on cultivating a good active listening practice.

Being an elite listener is worth it. Pause for a moment and think about the best listener you've ever experienced. I bet you have a very positive opinion of that person, whoever they are. We all have the chance to be any person's best listener.

Bill Clinton is often celebrated as being an elite listener. Whatever your opinion of the former president, he is famed for his ability to make whoever he is talking to feel like that most important person in the room, exactly what Marc trains his case officers to do. I'm certain that Bill Clinton was born with natural talents in this area. But I am equally certain that when he realized these skills could be a huge asset to him as a politician, he cultivated them until they were truly elite.

You've thought about your greatest listener, so let me tell you about mine.

Years ago, I joined a dinner with some colleagues, including one in particular who was a former CIA case officer based in the Middle East. He met his wife—who had the same job—while he was working in the region.

I sat next to her at dinner, and she was extraordinary. She was beautiful—she resembled a young Geena Davis—and that definitely helped things. Behavioral science shows that we are—for better or for worse—more positively disposed toward people we find attractive. But it was her incredible emotional intelligence that lingers with me when I think back to that dinner years ago.

She seemed to hang on every word I said, and encouraged me to share more, seemingly finding everything I said to be of great interest. She made steady (but not creepy) eye contact and appeared focused only on me, despite our rowdy table and the bustling surroundings. The result of it was that I found myself sharing a lot about myself, opening up in a very short period of time. I probably would have done just about anything she asked after speaking with her for an evening!

As an aside, when I reflect on the Young Geena Davis Spy, I think about how wise it was for the CIA to have her based in the Middle East, in some of the most conservative Gulf states. In these male-dominated cultures, men don't spend much time with women who aren't their wives, sisters, mothers—close family members. When they do spend time with these women, they tend to really open up. I'm certain that if the Young Geena Davis Spy was able to get just a bit of time with a Saudi minister or a Kuwaiti businessman, she would have been excellent at recruiting sources.

## LISTENING TIP: YOGA, MEDITATION, ETC.

I love yoga, hot yoga in particular. It helps me calm myself and stay in the moment.

When I'm in yoga class and in a difficult pose, I have to really concentrate to maintain the pose and my balance. If I allow mundane thoughts to intrude, or if I look around the room at others, I lose my balance.

But if I focus on my breathing, and maintain eye contact with myself in the mirror or with a fixed location in front of me, I am amazed at what my body can do and the progress I can make in my practice.

Yoga has helped me in conversation. When I'm talking to someone and I think of something that I'm dying to share in reply to what they are saying, I focus on my breath, I redouble my focus on my conversational counterpart. I remember that looking at what is going on around me instead of what I should be focusing on can cause me to lose my balance, which isn't a bad metaphor for losing track of a conversation because you're lost in your own thoughts.

Meditation has obvious parallels to this as well. But really, most sports and exercise can give you similar benefits—concentration, strengthening the ties between your mind and body, and being strategic with your actions.

The writer and monologist Spaulding Gray wrote about how skiing was liberating for him because it demanded his full attention, and so then he was free from the rampaging thoughts in his mind. Most sports demand intensity and concentration, the kind of focus that can really help you if you consciously try to bring some of that attentive discipline to your conversations. But really, anything that helps you get outside yourself and focus on something other than your thoughts—playing an instrument, gardening—can help improve your concentration and focus.

## MIRRORING

Mirroring is typically described as the replication of another person's nonverbal signals. It has been taught extensively in the business world, and perhaps you have even had some experience with it. I want to show you how spies use mirroring and offer a twist on this method that brings in the battle-tested experience of FBI hostage negotiators.

Let's dive into how you can consciously utilize this technique to build rapport and connect with your target.

A great starting point is to note that mirroring is very much a natural part of our lives, and indeed we use it from cradle to grave.

When we're babies, mirroring is a key component of our development. We watch the adults around us and how they behave, and we mimic them to literally learn how to be a human being.

It's a monkey-see, monkey-do kind of learning, and monkeys have actually been key to learning about mirroring in scientific studies.

In the 1990s, scientists discovered the existence of mirror neurons in the brain, primarily in the premotor cortex, when studying macaque monkeys. These areas of the brain are focused on evaluating the intentions and movements of others, in addition to motor planning and execution. Researchers noted that one's mirror neurons became active when that person was observing the actions or emotions of others.

Mirroring is something we continue to do subconsciously throughout our lives. Think about smiles. If someone smiles at you, isn't there a strong impulse to smile back? Or how about yawning? if someone leans back and yawns, you feel a desire to yawn as well (it almost feels contagious, right?). That is empathy at work, and empathy powers mirroring. We are naturally empathetic creatures. Mirroring brings us closer to each other.

The easiest mirroring technique for a business setting is what we'll call the "tabletop mirror." When you are sitting across the table from your target, and they have their arms on the table in a forward-leaning position, you should be in a similar position to mirror them. Don't sit back and assume a casual, relaxed posture. If they are smiling frequently, smile back; if they have a more serious expression, mirror that. If they are using hand gestures, when you're responding to them use your hands a bit more than you normally would. You get the idea.

Some believe that you should monitor your target's breathing and try to mirror their breathing rate. It may subconsciously make you more connected to your target. Others believe that even mirroring your target's blink rate is something to try. Such thoughts are nice enough, but they've always seemed like overkill to me. There are factors that might impact these behaviors that have nothing to do with one's mental state. For blink rate, someone could have just put in contact lenses, or there could be dust in the air. Similarly, someone's breathing rate could be the result of a health condition and not about anticipation or anxiety. But it's worth noting how far some people take mirroring.

While physical mirroring is often taught to businesspeople, I consider verbal mirroring the executive-level move—a powerful way to augment your connection strategy, especially when layered on top of physical mirroring.

Verbal mirroring is a key tool in the tool kit of FBI hostage negotiators. Think about the challenge a hostage negotiator faces. There's an angry man (it's always a man) who has taken at least one hostage. Often, he's already committed an act of violence, perhaps even killed someone. He's agitated, and potentially mentally ill. A hostage negotiator can't be seated across from the hostage-taker—connection is usually just by a phone or a walkie-talkie, so they can't read the hostage-taker's body language and try to mirror it to stroke the hostage-taker's subconscious and signal understanding.

A hostage negotiator relies on verbal mirroring to help connect with the hostage-taker. The use of verbal mirroring is a critical piece of trying to calm the situation and bring it to a resolution without violence.

The hostage negotiator listens for words from the hostage-taker that can be spoken back to that person because—just like with physical mirroring—our brains recognize the words they just heard come out of our mouths, signaling understanding and empathy. Furthermore, a good hostage negotiator will look for *pet words* or certain colloquial expressions to use back to the hostage-taker.

Think about it. Don't you have certain words or sayings that you tend to repeat, that become almost a part of your personality? I have a friend who says "one hundred percent" when they want to affirm something; another says "by the way" frequently as a verbal crutch. When I'm speaking with them, I often say these phrases back to them because even though they are good friends and we already have rapport built up, it helps me to practice my mirroring chops, and it has honestly become somewhat second nature. A hostage negotiator, and a smart sales professional, can benefit from being on the lookout for these types of words and phrases. Subtly including them when they are speaking back to their counterpart is an effective tactic.

Perhaps a client says the following in a meeting:

"I like how your software could help us streamline how we view our supply chain; visibility into where our products are at any moment is a constant struggle. But it's early days in our budgeting for the next fiscal year, so we're going to have to put a pin in this for now."

Sales professionals tend to nicely sum things up and will say toward the end of the meeting something like "What I'm hearing from you is that your budget for next year isn't yet clear; and while you like how our software could potentially fit in next year, it's too soon to move forward."

That's fine as far as it goes, and summarizing things to make sure you're all on the same page is surely not a bad idea. If you practice that already, you're on your way toward incorporating some of the emotion labeling we're going to get into. But I'm talking about something else.

Utilizing verbal mirroring here would be more subtle, so use the same language the target used to reinforce subconsciously how well you have listened and how tuned-in you are. It will support making the sale.

Try this:

"I get that it's early days when it comes to the next fiscal year's budget, but I'm really glad to hear you see how we might be able to help you streamline your supply chain and help provide more visibility into your distribution partners. I'll put a pin in it on my side as well, and we'll circle back in a few weeks."

Replying in this way is superior because you're not only demonstrating that you have heard them, but also that you understand their challenge, and you are not going to pressure them to make a decision that they are not yet ready for. You have also subtly utilized key words they used—"streamline your supply-chain partners," "visibility," "fiscal year"—to subconsciously build rapport. But even more important, you recognized and utilized the *pet words* that the client used—"early days" and "put a pin in it" are likely part of their regular colloquialisms. You have signaled to their brain that you are on the same page.

The language used by your target is often a key element of their culture. Some businesses operate on a calendar year for their budget cycle; others have their own calendars that dictate their fiscal cycle; and that distinction governs much about how they decide things. Terms like "streamline" might be buzzwords within their company, and subtlety picking that up and utilizing it can make it seem like you're a part of the team, that you get them. It can offer a degree of influence when it comes time for your counterpart to choose between your service or another vendor.

An extra word of caution when it comes to mirroring, picking up on what we learned from the map anecdote:

Mirroring is a subtle skill, and you should practice this in your everyday life, as I do with the friends I mentioned. Mirroring is in fact the most important of the skills to practice, because when it is done poorly it can be a disaster. Badly executed mirroring can look like you're copying or, even worse, mocking someone. Obviously, that's the opposite of your goal for anyone you're mirroring, who you are trying, of course, to win over and influence.

So practice both forms of mirroring in your everyday life, make it almost second nature in how you interact with people, and get truly comfortable with it before you bring it into the more high-stakes interactions of your career.

## KEY TAKEAWAYS

When looking to connect with and influence someone, there are plenty of opportunities to showcase your dazzling personality, but sometimes the best thing you can do is nothing—close your mouth and just listen. When you do speak, be strategic and deliberate about how you gather information and handle your body language and tone of voice.

1. Elicitation offers us a way to gather information about our targets that avoids excessive questioning, which can often engender the opposite response we are after. Remember that triggered responses, like the tendency to correct and reactions to flattery, can often be the pathway to collect vital intelligence. Use the violin conversation when engaged in a premeditated attempt to elicit information.

2. Active listening is the most important skill that any spy or salesperson can cultivate. Overcome the evolutionary challenges related to listening by being aware of those natural impediments. Be the rare person who remembers a person's name after meeting them, and use that name in conversation to demonstrate respect.

3. Exercise of almost any sort, and quite a few other hobbies, can be a great way to improve your concentration and focus on the task at hand, rather than just focusing on your inner thoughts.

4.  Mirroring offers a shortcut to rapport-building by leveraging our natural instincts. Verbal mirroring provides another level of signaling to your counterpart that you're on the same page with them.

5.  Practice these subtle skills in your everyday life in order to get comfortable with them in more low-stakes environments than your career. Many of these skills can backfire if they are done poorly!

# 3

# ESPIONAGE AND ENVIRONMENT

*How Spies Leverage Culture and Diversity to Win*

I have demonstrated how spies utilize specialized strategies to connect with their targets, and I've shown how you can do so, as well. Now, I'll share some spycraft that will help you improve your networking skills, be a better manager of people, and build teams that are positioned to succeed.

## ATMOSPHERE AND INTANGIBLES

When I came back from China, the first job I took in New York was with one of the "Big Four" global accounting firms. I was on their specialized China-focused team.

I found the office atmosphere stifling and depressing. Complaining about the endless rows of anonymous cubicles one time to a colleague, I got a wake-up call. "Clients don't want to visit our firm and see amazing interior design," he said. "Sure, these days we provide a lot of different consulting services, but at its heart this company is an accounting firm: that's its culture. Clients come in here and want to see bean-counters at work, not amazing art."

That really stuck with me and has influenced how I sell. The environment in which we're connecting and influencing should directly impact the approach we're taking to connect and influence. Spies understand this and utilize their surroundings to their advantage. Let's discuss ways for you to do so.

Here are two different scenarios for a prospect pitch.

Scenario A: You're waiting in a conference room for your prospects. It's a staid room without adornment, with a view of a parking lot. You think you hear the shuffling of feet coming down the hallway, but no voices. They walk in quietly, almost glum, not talking at all amongst themselves: three older men, conservatively dressed. They sit down at the conference table, and while getting settled give you the most cursory of greetings. Then it's right down to business.

Scenario B: This conference room has pictures from the company's most recent annual off-sites. You take a look at the photos and see a montage of team-building exercises, colleagues laughing in a tug-of-war contest, playing softball, and zip-lining. You review the smiling faces and then quickly get to your seat as you hear voices coming down the hall. You hear several people laughing, and then they walk into the room teasing one member of the group about something he said at the team happy hour that they have attended the night before, all pretty amused by this recollection. They sit down at the table and fill you in on what happened the night before, making small talk with you for a while before you realize it's almost ten minutes past the start time of the meeting and you haven't even gotten started talking business.

Pretty different scenarios for a salesperson to encounter, right? I think we'd all agree that tailoring your approach for the different groups is the smart thing to do. You would do this naturally, subconsciously, as we do in all social situations.

But let's elevate our evaluation of these two situations. Let's make your response to these highly different scenarios a conscious act and shape your approach as a result. I want you to take the subconscious to the conscious level.

A little later, we're going to talk about how labeling works when it comes to defusing tense encounters and in negotiation. Here, I want to foreshadow that and put my own twist on it.

The human brain is a marvel, and when we encounter the two different situations I've described, the brain will help us to subconsciously pivot to navigate each one. We tend to join the social norms that are being established around us, and in these cases we will conform to the social norms that our prospects have established. Taking that to a *conscious* level can help you to use the Atmosphere and Intangibles to further your goals.

I want you to label these situations as the meeting gets started.

Scenario A: *These are serious, sober people who clearly value a truly professional environment. I should demonstrate my professionalism, get to my value proposition quickly, and utilize concrete examples about how my company can help support theirs.*

Scenario B: *These people care about having fun in their work. They're proud that they enjoy working together and clearly put a lot of emphasis on team-building. If I can show that I fit into that paradigm, and that I could even enhance it by adding my own fun personality to the mix, I could be more successful in my pitch. I'm going to let my personality shine and really develop my personal rapport with this team.*

Articulating in your mind what atmosphere you're operating in can solidify your approach to rapport-building and pitching, much in the same way that when you take a note it helps you remember it internally, not just on paper. You don't have to note as much as I've just done above; it can be as quick as *fun group, let's show them how I fit in.* That internal monologue propels you toward what spies do best: using everything around you to find the best ways to connect with your targets.

Of course, it doesn't end once those prospects sit down.

Once seated, are you detecting any rivalry at the table? Are any of the potential clients vying for control, seeking to run the meeting and to describe what their needs are in a slightly different way than the other(s)?

Maybe you have targeted the attendee with the most senior title, the managing director, as the key person to influence. But at the meeting the managing director is playing with her phone nearly the whole time, being quite rude, actually, and not paying you much attention. The principal,* seated next to her, is the most engaged, asking the most pertinent questions. You can determine that she will decide on your pitch, and the managing director will likely just sign the contract.

These are the Atmosphere and Intangibles, and I'm a huge believer in how they can impact sales. The Atmosphere and Intangibles are all the details that you might not think have anything specifically to do with the sale you're trying to make, but in fact prove important to achieving that goal. They include everything from the personalities of your clients to what their office looks like to what kind of culture they cultivate. A smart salesperson, just like a crafty spy, will take note of these details to gain any advantage they can. Let's talk about how to do it.

Spies absolutely think carefully about the atmosphere they are operating in and how to proceed with their mission. Marc Polymeropoulos recalls that an Agency colleague would "walk into a station and know whether it was a high-performing station. He called it a soul. He could discern whether a team was

---

* In the world of finance or corporate consulting, the managing director or partner is often top dog. Just below them are principals, senior associates, and associates, though of course some firms vary in their titles.

high-performing and motivated by how the office looked and felt. It's a feel, the soul of the station, you can feel the energy. That first impression was something he talked about."

Be mindful of all the atmospheric and inter-relational details. Jot them down on paper, even. It can pay dividends for the smart account executive. Even if the behavior you're noting doesn't impact the short-term prospect of the sale, paying attention and noting these details are part of the long game that can differentiate a successful salesperson from an average one.

We've discussed how Atmosphere and Intangibles go beyond just human behavior to include what the actual office looks like.

If I go on a sales pitch and the client's office is spartan (like the former accounting firm I worked for), with seemingly very little effort put into dressing up the space, I note that fact and I think that a value sell is likely the way to go—they are more likely to be very conscious of their budget. So if I can adjust my pitch to focus on the thrift and comparative value of my product or service, I'll have a higher likelihood of success.

Alternatively, if I go on a sales pitch and the office is beautiful, with high-end furniture and tasteful, carefully chosen art on the walls, I tend to think that a premium sell—anchoring the pitch on what I'm selling being the best of the best—is the approach to take.

Pat Donegan, former senior managing director of sales excellence at the Riverside Company, explains the different goals: "Simply put, a value or 'price' sale is between customers/buyers who are motivated by getting the best price possible. They are cost conscious and their goal is affordability/budget and products and services in this category are commodity-like with low switching costs between providers. Alternatively, a premium sale occurs between custom-ers/buyers who are willing to pay more for differentiated 'value' for product or service. They are focused on high quality—even scarce offerings that enable achievement of personal or high priority busi-ness goals such as growth, innovation, or competitive advantage."

The atmosphere of your potential buyer's office can direct you toward the right sales approach.

Now let's look beyond the office environment and even beyond how your targets exist within their own worlds. How do these potential clients present themselves to the world?

A former case officer once remarked to me: "People wear their identities and often tell you who they are."

Spies know that how people present themselves to the world— how they dress, their hairstyle, facial hair, etc.—is an advertise-ment about those people, a key to unlocking how to approach and cultivate them. According to John Sipher, "there is information always there to look at and think through" when meeting some-one for the first time and making initial assessments. "Our initial instincts are usually right—not always, but usually. You can see for yourself whether they are trying to give off an impression that they are outgoing or maybe show where they're from. There are all sorts of things you can take away about someone just by observing them initially: are they inward-looking, are they talking about their job, their family, etc.? You notice if they look a certain way, in particular if it doesn't quite fit in. You might think to yourself how you know a bunch of people from the country this person is from, but this guy seems to be different in terms of what he might be wearing or how he is conducting himself. As a case officer, that is interesting for us—we are looking for people like that who might not fit in and might be frustrated. Those people tend to be easiest to recruit."

I know an FBI agent who agrees with this CIA case officer. Joe Navarro, the FBI expert on body language, believes that human beings are quite readable. Joe can cite repeated studies that have validated this fact with accuracy ratings consistently over 75 percent when it comes to making precise assessments about people from afar. He points to research done by social psychologist Nalini Ambady showing that we correctly assess people within 3 milliseconds.

Joe points out that this makes evolutionary sense. When cavepeople were roaming the plains, we learned to make quick judgments about other people, animals, and situations. If ancient humans had been slower, they could have met a bad fate.

People don't just subtly advertise who they are through their appearance—they shout it out! It's all there in our haircuts and facial hair (or lack thereof), our choice of glasses, watches, jewelry, and other accessories; it's apparent in our choice of clothing and how we wear it. It is further described in our body language and tone of voice. All these details are advertisements for who we are and, just as importantly, how we want the world to see us. A spy will utilize these advertisements to determine who they talk to and how they make their approach. You should, too.

That's why I tell clients and audiences that you *can* judge a book by its cover! The key disclaimer is that the initial judgment is just a hypothesis. Just like a spy, you should trust your intuition and instincts about someone and make your choices about *whether* to approach them and *how* to approach them accordingly. But don't be wedded to that initial impression. Be ready to be contradicted.

*"Do I contradict myself? Very well, then,*
*I contradict myself. I am large, I contain multitudes."*
—Walt Whitman

Human beings are full of contradictions. We all have different sides of our personalities, and we often shift to different aspects of those personalities very quickly (a skill we're going to work on a bit later, in fact).

That's why, while I suggest you trust your initial impression of someone—and make the choice of who and how to approach accordingly—you must be ready for that person to surprise you. If you're stuck on someone's initial appearance as a real square, and suddenly they show themselves as actually being unconventional in their interests and personality, you're potentially going to blow the rapport-building process.

## SPIES AND DIVERSITY

Diversity is a huge buzzword in corporate life at the moment. Part of a rising set of metrics that investors, customers, and prospective employees are using to evaluate a company, it has led to executives scrambling to showcase a wider set of humanity within boards and C-suites, and indeed throughout organizations. Regardless of whether you think this is a good movement that properly addresses the inequities of the past or is political correctness run amok, diversity initiatives are not likely to fade away anytime soon.

The CIA and other government agencies involved in national security and law enforcement look at diversity in slightly more utilitarian terms. They have found that using different types of people in different cultures can lead to better outcomes for missions and have therefore embraced the notion of diversity. Leveraging a diverse team is another area where we can refocus on how we view a particular issue through the lens of elite government employees.

First, let's challenge the notion that diversity is just about having a variety of skin colors, genders, and ethnicities on a team.

Those things surely matter, but diversity—in the end—is about the experience and skill sets that those people bring. Spies know that having a team of people that look and think the same way is not an advantage when it comes to accomplishing difficult and often clandestine missions.

Even though Greg Roberts is a white man from Oklahoma, he views his recruitment to the CIA as being a diversity hire. While the CIA has grown more multicultural over recent decades, when Greg joined, it was still shaking off its legacy as being the domain of elite, upper-class white men who went to Ivy League universities.

"I was a farm boy out of the military. I didn't have a similar background to those East Coast Ivy Leaguers who mostly grew up in large cities. That might have made it harder to fit in to the Agency at that time, but my background made it easier to get to know a lot of people that I wound up needing to connect with. Many of the countries I served in are like the U.S. was pre–World War II when people were just coming off the farms to the cities. They had strong ties to the countryside, just like I did, and I understood that it influenced their thought patterns, the concerns that they have, and the way that they approach life. There's a certain type of insecurity you think about with that rural background, how the weather can wipe you out, how you look at the future; it helped me make a connection with agents I recruited.

"I'm not trying to be self-aggrandizing, but I really felt that I was a diversity hire because it's not what you look like—that's the most shallow way to look at diversity—it's about different understandings and competencies."

Marc Polymeropoulos would likely agree. He tells a story about a team-building exercise that shows the value of having members with varied backgrounds. The story he tells of a team-building exercise showcases how diversity is about deeper skill sets as much as it is about outward appearance.

"Whenever I would put together a new team of case officers, I would gather everyone and ask them to go around in the group and share one thing about themselves that had nothing to do with work. When I gathered this particular team together for this exercise, I was just looking for ways to break the ice and get the team to know each other so everyone would cooperate better. What I ultimately found was someone on my team with a particular skill and background that led directly to an important recruitment.

"As we made our way around the room, one young female member of the team told everyone that she played Division I soccer. She didn't brag about it, but it turned out that she had been a big deal in college.

"So the station had dossiers on many of the diplomats of interest from certain countries we target, and it turned out that a diplomat from one of our toughest adversaries stationed in the same city was a huge soccer fan, including at the collegiate level. So I had an idea about how to work with that.

"I organized a friendly soccer match between embassy staffs, and we invited this diplomatic mission to play. I hoped that this particular soccer-mad diplomat would take the bait and find playing in the game irresistible, and that was exactly what happened.

"He recognized our soccer star and was delighted to meet her and compete against her. She had her orders, and at the reception after the game she hit it off with the diplomat and began a relationship that ultimately led to sustained and productive contact with a very elusive diplomat."

Marc's usage of his soccer star wasn't only about having a woman on a team that historically has been comprised of WASPY male Coastal elites. It was about leveraging a woman's particular experience and skill set to allow her to make a particular contribution. There was no one else on Marc's team who could have recruited that agent in such an effective way. "You have to use the best-athlete approach," Marc summed up, enjoying the double meaning in this case.

Marc points to the Middle East for other examples of how spies leverage diversity. Do you remember the Young Geena Davis Spy—my greatest listener? Well, she wasn't a one-off for the Agency by any means. It turns out that the CIA uses women in particular in these conservative Gulf countries, despite the rampant misogynism.

Remember when I noted how in the Arab world men confide in the women in their lives? Well, it's not the only advantage that female spies possess in these male-dominated cultures. Women in the Muslim world are often covered head to toe in identity-shielding outfits, which makes detection by security harder and aids in security-detection runs (SDRs). Because of this, the Agency often uses female case officers to handle some of their most sensitive agents in this region.

Marc pointed out additional ways that the Agency uses diversity to exploit other societal prejudices in the Middle East. For instance, in many of the megacities of the Gulf, Filipinos are brought in to do low-level construction and domestic work. Because this work is low status, these people are often treated as afterthoughts by Arab security, who don't really pay attention to them in the same way that they would with, say, a white man. So an Asian-American case officer can operate almost invisibly in these Gulf megacities and go to places that white men might not be able to without drawing the attention of the authorities.

So the Agency has flipped prejudices to exploit the ugly weakness often found in them. The practice shows how diversity on teams is a matter of strength, not just image.

General Stanley McChrystal has learned similar lessons in the course of his storied career serving in the U.S. military. A four-star general when he retired and widely considered one of the greatest military minds of his generation, he watched as diversity became a matter of evolution and practical tradecraft rather than some mandate that the military had to implement.

Earlier in his career, he noted that in "counterterrorism forces the only diversity was whether you had blond hair because otherwise everyone kind of looked the same with their big muscles and all of that. But we learned some things. We found out that there are places where one man alone would stand out, which we obviously didn't want. But if you put what appeared to be a married couple in the same location it wouldn't draw the same attention, so we brought women in" and created small counterterrorism units of men and women posing as married couples.

"Then we started to find out that women were actually really good at what they did. We learned that they were less threatening to certain people. Anytime you get people out of the stereotype of what they expect, the more you get away from that you can engage differently. If you're a fit middle-aged man, you might have one way of thinking of something—it's like that expression that if you're holding a hammer everything looks like a nail. If you don't have that, you think of language and other ways to solve problems—you use a much different set of solutions for a problem. Ultimately the more subtle the mission, the more important that becomes."

Matthew Horace is a twenty-eight-year veteran of federal, state, and local law enforcement, and a prominent Chief Security Officer for major international corporations. He finished his career in the prestigious position of special agent in charge in the Senior Executive Service of the United States Department of Justice. Matt's experience as a black man in law enforcement and now in top positions in corporate America has made him a highly sought-after voice on diversity issues.

"High-performing teams and diverse teams are interchange-able. If you have a multidimensional team prepared for a variety of scenarios, you're ahead of the game. There is more capacity to execute more things more often than if you don't have that diverse team around the table. Working for the U.S. government, you used to call in the exact people that you need for a particular assign-ment. But in corporate America, they are finally learning that if you have a diverse team and they are all high-performing people, you're going to get better results faster."

But according to Matt, corporate America is also awakening to the fact that it's not only about better execution on tasks, it's about risk management. "Organizations miss a cue in a marketing cam-paign and it's because no one at the table was diverse enough to call something out. So then the product hits the market, and a big crisis results and people wonder how it could happen."

What makes diversity hard is that we are all more positively predisposed toward people that resemble us, that have similar stories to us. This is hardwired in people, and understanding that is the key to getting started on unlocking the advantages of creating diverse teams. Because ultimately diverse teams offer many unique options to advance the mission. At its heart, diversity is leveraging the unique experiences and backgrounds of a team to think about problem-solving and other issues from different perspectives. If we only hire people we're immediately comfortable with because they mirror our background and worldview, we're losing out on so much creative thinking and a variety of helpful perspectives. We also miss out on the chance to utilize different ethnicities and genders to target different groups as part of any mission.

You might think that the Secret Service would be a strange place to find a model for diversity. Secret Service agents all cultivate the same aesthetic in public—dark sunglasses, unsmiling, serious, straight-backed. It's as if they were cut from a mold—and you might think that they were minted from a law-enforcement background that prioritized physical intimidation and violence suppression.

In fact, Secret Service agents take a great deal of pride in their agency's original investigative mandate. Founded in 1865, the Service was a branch of the U.S. Treasury with a mission to combat the counterfeiting of U.S. currency. That legacy continues today, with most Secret Service agents starting off in field offices where they gain experience on investigative matters.

Mark Sullivan took this path in a career that ultimately led him to be head of the Secret Service. He was in the Agency's Detroit field office for seven years, working on investigations, before he moved up the ladder. He is a big believer in the fact that Secret Service agents have a wealth of experience dealing with all sorts of people before they are charged with managing the likes of a U.S. president or vice president.

"I think that there is a real advantage to having different perceptions. Having a different view on something comes from having a different experience. That's what diversity brings, whether it's gender or race or what you've done in your career. If you can have that combination of different ages, different types of things that people have done in their careers—that kind of diversity of thought is a really valuable thing. It's good to bring someone in who had done something different in their career."

I find it ironic that while much of corporate America is ostensibly pursuing a diverse workforce, in some ways they are strangling the type of diversity that Mark cites, which helps make the Secret Service so good at what they do.

Apply for a job in corporate America today, and your résumé is likely to first go through a software program that will use AI to screen you out if you, for instance, don't have the requisite number of years doing a particular type of job. Leaders think that for a senior sales job, you need at least a decade in a similar role.

But what if someone with a winning personality, who knows a lot about the product or service the company is selling (maybe they were a customer), who lived overseas and has an abundance of experience influencing people, applies for the job. They get a form rejection because they didn't fit the rather parochial view of what the human resources team, in conjunction with team leaders, has set up for the profile of the job.

Because of their narrow definition of who is right for the job, that team will miss out on people who can bring their own unique background, a point of view that by virtue of being different could provide so much.

## TAKING NOTES LIKE A SPY

We've spent some time going over details about how to assess the personalities of the clients you're trying to influence, how their cultures can play a strong role in how you should approach selling to them, and how composing your own sales team with diversity can help your company win. A critical aspect of utilizing these details is understanding that they are subtle—in the midst of a busy week of sales meetings, you might forget them. That's why note-taking is such a strong part of the plan to leverage the Atmosphere and Intangibles to reach your goals.

Spies are expert note-takers. No agent gets recruited without extensive notes on the target. Oftentimes the recruitment of an agent begins with an extensive dossier of information on the target with notes on their particular situation. For example, the CIA might have assessed that the target has a young child with a disease that is difficult to treat in their authoritarian, impoverished country. But the U.S. might have much more advanced medical resources for such a disease, which could offer hope to the diplomat from this adversarial country that, if they were to cooperate, the U.S. would relocate their family and pay for their child's medical care.

One former case officer with a wealth of experience working on recruiting such targets points out: "The thing you are being judged on most is your assessment of the target. So the operational cables with your notes on the target are enormously important. It's deliberative; you have to put it all down on paper, the whole process of getting someone over the line. After you meet someone, the first thing you do is write up everything about them."

Note-taking has always been a part of my work DNA because I started my career as a journalist. Speaking to someone and developing a shorthand of what they are saying and later reviewing it were absolutely essential parts of my journalistic tradecraft. The key quotes for my story were obviously of paramount importance, but I also got into the habit of noting the intangible details, such as how they said something, the environment in which we spoke, etc.

Note-taking continued to be a big part of my professional life even after I left journalism and entered the corporate world. What is clear to me is that it is currently a blind spot in corporate life, and I think it's one of the areas that clearly should be improved. I've joined several well-known global consultancies and been handed multi-million-dollar books of business and been given little to no context on these clients. The best I could find out about these new clients of mine was some scuttlebutt from the team, but basically nothing on who the individuals were at the account and what they were like.

This is a huge weak point in most sales organizations, a huge detriment considering that sales has one of the highest turnover rates amongst white-collar jobs. Salespeople regularly leave jobs or get laid off; and, because organizations do a rather poor job of instituting note-taking requirements for their team, they leave with precious institutional memory. The new sales rep essentially has to start from scratch, or something close to it.

If I were joining a company as the new head of sales, the first thing I would do would be to implement a rule that all meetings and calls must be memorialized in detail in the Client Relationship Management (CRM) system. I would seek to create a detailed log of the account that over time would reveal an insightful picture of the client and its culture. Think about the huge advantage of having years of notes on a client, its key contacts, the way the client company has fared during the ups and downs of its history, the way the relationship between your firm and the client company has navigated the inevitable ups and downs of any relationship. Now think about not having any of that and plugging a new sales rep in with a client your firm has had for years with the most cursory of details available about that history, and it'll be clear to you that having detailed notes is a great way to maintain and grow a client.

As your head of sales, all my account reps would be required to note things such as: What are the key individuals like at the client? Do they have kids? Where do they vacation? Where did they go to school? What sports teams do they follow? When are their birthdays? Any and all details essentially on the key people who are influential at the client company.

What is the client office like (value or premium sell)? What are they like as a group in their office? Do they show different behavior when you get them out of the office for a meal or a drink? Are there any charities they support?

These are details that can play a critical role in winning and/or holding on to a client. A salesperson that knows the birthday of a client and the names of her kids, and remembers to ask about how their weekend was at their lake house, is a salesperson who has a better chance at influencing their client than one who doesn't.

And the salesperson who has those details already in the company CRM system is one who has a greater chance at success than one who doesn't.

I always say that unless your product or service is truly differentiated, or your product or service has a price point that blows competitors out of the water, it is salesmanship that makes the critical difference. Most markets are competitive—there isn't all that much difference between a few different providers' products or services—so how a client feels about their salesperson can be all the difference in winning or retaining a client. Good intelligence—as spies know and show all the time in their work—can make all the difference in distinguishing you from your competitor.

Many spies are natural note-takers. They have detail-oriented, analytical minds, and that is augmented with training to help them observe and then capture minutiae that might contribute to their cause. A case officer who finishes meeting with an agent will immediately set to work sending what's called an after-action report noting all of the details. They don't just note the intelligence they get from their agent. They also note the agent's mindset, what's going on in their life, whether they might be under increased suspicion, and a range of other details. Basically the Atmosphere and Intangibles, just as a salesperson should note these things in addition to what kind of budget the client might have, when a proposal should be sent, etc.

I was somewhat infamous with my colleagues because I would leave a meeting, and as soon as it was appropriate I wanted to note everything about the meeting, which would annoy my colleagues, especially if they were more on the research side than the account management side. But I insisted on doing it because I was following the tradecraft of intelligence officers who I knew were taking such detailed notes, and I saw these details serve me well as I developed a reputation for growing strong relationships with my clients at the multiple jobs I've had over the years.

What about note-taking during a meeting? When I'm actually in a meeting, yes, I do take notes, but there are several things to point out. First, taking notes when someone is talking can be interpreted as respectful, which is of course something I'm trying to do in a meeting and when I'm developing a relationship generally. If someone sees you note down something they say, they know that you were listening carefully and that you thought it was important and it inflates their self-esteem. I will sometimes note something in a meeting that I don't think is that important, but that I can tell that the person is proud of, to utilize that tendency.

But generally speaking, I keep the note-taking in meetings somewhat minimal, looking to build regard in the way I just described or to capture something very specific such as a budget number or date when a proposal might be due. In the meeting itself, I want to be practicing my active-listening skills, making good eye contact, mirroring behavior, and eliciting information that could be helpful. It's my after-action report, which I then go file in the CRM, that is of utmost importance.

Another good strategy, this one employed by FBI hostage negotiators, is to have one person as the designated note-taker at the meeting if you're not alone in attending a client meeting. You can't really listen and take notes at once: our brains are limited-capacity processors. That's one of the reasons I take sparse notes in meetings and do that brain dump afterward. The FBI knows this and therefore doesn't ask its negotiators to take notes in high-pressure environments when they are focused on ways to build rapport and trying to bring a standoff to an end. Taking a colleague along, perhaps a junior member of the team, just to take detailed notes is a winning strategy, especially if they've been trained in observing and noting the Atmosphere and Intangibles. Afterward, when you've done your own brain dump, you can literally compare notes and have an even better record of what transpired and what levers you might pull to grow that account.

I've mentioned how much of an advantage it can be for salespeople to have detailed records of the accounts they are working on, because if the account has to transition to someone new they can hit the ground running.

The importance of note-taking is even more acute in the world of espionage. Case officers only handle an agent for a few years before turning the agent over to someone new. There are many reasons for this. Case officers are frequently based in challenging parts of the world, and the Agency doesn't want to burn out their officers, or put their families through too much hardship, by stationing them indefinitely in some of these places. And while the CIA trains its case officers on how to build rapport and get close to their targets, it is wary of those relationships going on for too long and becoming too personal. The Agency doesn't want case officers to get too close to an agent. This rule of thumb is tough for both case officer and agent, because a special relationship often develops due to the illicit nature of their work. As Marc Polymouropolous shared, sometimes an agent will tell a case officer that they are only spying because of that relationship.

When an agent is turned over to a new case officer, that detailed record of the agent—what it took to recruit the agent, what their motivations were, how the relationship has gone, what the agent's family is like and what they know or don't know about their spying—all has an important bearing on how they are handled by the new case officer.

The corollaries with sales are hopefully now clear. Use every tool at your disposal to safeguard and grow your relationships, just as a good case officer would do when the stakes are much higher. Note-taking should be an essential tool in your tool kit to do exactly that.

## CULTURAL CONTEXT: "BY, WITH, THROUGH"

I spent quite a while walking you through the value of elicitation—collecting information in a more circumspect manner—and how that can lead to unique insights and open up subtle pathways to guide you forward on your sales mission.

But I want to throw a curveball at you and talk about candor for a moment as we discuss how cultural context should be considered in the sales world and how we can look to the military's special forces community for inspiration.

The culture I was born into is that of a New Yorker. We're known to be straightforward, wearing our hearts on our sleeves, and you know where you stand with us. We're famous for it! I love that about my culture and my friends, family, and colleagues would likely tell you that I very much embody that.

While elicitation offers us some amazing chances to collect intelligence, candor can be a great method of getting to the heart of the matter, demonstrating respect, and showing that you're honest.

In a sales environment, unfortunately our targets often have their guard up and have a heightened sense of the tactics that you might be using on them. Candor can disarm that by cutting right to the heart of the matter. Candor on your team encourages a culture of transparency; it can save time and reduce miscommunication.

As a candid New Yorker who values that trait in my own interactions, I found living in China to be hard.

To say that candor is not a trait common to the Chinese is an understatement. No one wants to tell you no, for starters, so you lose a lot of time listening to your counterparts dance around a negative instead of just being honest with you. If you get annoyed because no one will level with you about things, they tend to smile somewhat embarrassedly, which always made me feel ridiculous (which I probably was).

I had a hard time remembering that within the country's cultural disposition, I was the outlier here. Culturally, the Chinese valued different things in interpersonal interaction than what I had grown up with in New York. At more introspective times, I told myself I could adapt or suffer. I confess, I did a lot of suffering.

China is an extreme example, but understanding culture—or at least respecting the differences of our varied cultures—will help you better navigate people who don't see the world as you do, who don't react to it in ways that make the most sense to you. That's true if you do any sort of traveling beyond your immediate microculture, even if it's not quite as far as China.

Intelligence officers have to build deep relationships with people from all over the world, every culture imaginable. They think deeply about where a person is from, what shaped them into who they are, and seek to understand the prevailing cultural habits (like the Chinese smiling at furious foreigners).

In addition to considering the cultural context of where that person is from and what shaped them, let's return to the question of motivation. A spy might find out that the target is a government official who has been passed over for promotions many times by people much less talented than they are but are from the favored ethnic group or tribe—and the passed-over one is not. A good spy will keep that motivation in mind, along with the cultural context, as they are doing their recruitment, just like the NOC case officer I worked with when he understood the Chinese cultural tradition of seeking the best education possible for their children.

As a salesperson, your mission is to do the same thing.

Culturally, let's say you're an East Coaster, more specifically a Northeasterner like me, and your client is a typical Midwesterner. Midwesterners tend to be much more averse to conflict, to be more circumspect when sharing their opinions than those of us from the Northeast. It would behoove you to understand literally where your prospect is coming from as you, say, await word on your proposal. If you call or email aggressively to get that answer, you will likely engender a negative response because culturally you're pushing against the grain of what this person is used to. (You'll also confirm the negative stereotypes about where you're from and what salespeople are all about.)

Instead, build time and understanding into your sales cycle. Know that if the client is located in the Midwest, and in your discussions seems like the laid-back type who won't treat your proposal like the hot-button issue you believe it is (trying to hit your quarterly quota, etc.), patience will give you a better chance of success.

The vaunted world of military Special Forces (SF) has lessons for those of us in business who need to interact with people from different cultures, whether that is the hard-charging Northeasterner doing business in the Midwest, or an investor exploring opportunities in the Middle East. The slogan *By, With, Through* is something of a bumper sticker for SF, a central philosophy orienting these elite warriors' approach to the understanding of local cultures. It leads to collaboration and success. The philosophy of By, With, Through seeks to understand local culture and collaborate with members of the local population to achieve a mission. The concept, as we shall see, can be applied to a salesperson, or to anyone trying to influence and cooperate with someone from a different culture.

The SF, like the CIA, are a relatively new creation for the U.S. government. It was only after World War II that the U.S. established these groups of select war fighters, based in part on the United Kingdom's successful deployment of their Special Boat Teams and other small groups.

"It all starts with selection," according to famed Lieutenant General John F. Mulholland Jr. A leader in the SF community for decades, including as a member of the revered Delta Forces, General Mulholland eventually achieved the position of commander of the United States Army Special Operations Command. He also served as associate director for military affairs (ADMA) at the CIA, so he knows the world of spies as well. General Mulholland points out that the SF was the first organization for which the U.S. government used behavioral scientists in the selection of individuals—"they were looking for men who could work cooperatively with someone from a foreign culture. The behavioral scientists observed the candidates throughout the process to see if they were showing signs that might disqualify them (impatience, doesn't work well with others); after that process we had a high degree of confidence we're going to have the right person, but they were still assessing to make sure we didn't miss something and to see if they were a fit. Of course you need to do all the military stuff, but being a force multiplier by working with indigenous forces is a special skill," and one that was an essential part of this kind of warrior's makeup.

General Mulholland points out that in recent decades of continuous war in Afghanistan and Iraq, the SF community had moved away from this focus on collaboration with indigenous forces. The pace of warfare meant that teams like the SEALs and Delta (mostly known as "The Unit") were focused more on carrying out raids to kill bad guys than on establishing bonds with locals to find longer-term solutions to the problems causing violence. "The SF guys realized it was fun to be a commando, and they are really good at that. It became less about working with local forces." General

Mulholland is retired now, but he still has a finger on the pulse of the community that he served with for so long. "The commando stuff is still sexy, but the SF are now in the process of getting back to the roots of *By, With, Through.*"

Before the SF community became focused on the commando aspect of their work, General Mulholland led a team of highly trained warriors leveraging their skills of collaboration and cultural understanding to achieve one of the most important U.S. military wins in recent history.

When 9/11 happened, the team was quickly called upon because of its focus on the Middle East. Yes, the team's regional focus included Afghanistan, but the problem was that General Mulholland's people had focused for years on the threats arising from some of the more well-known adversaries in the Middle East, not the fringe of Central Asia. They were aware of bin Laden, his threats, and his history of violence against the U.S., and his presence in Afghanistan, but at the time Afghanistan was considered more of a backwater country with a low threat level. The effectiveness of the attacks of 9/11 was truly due to surprise and the unconventional tactics that the terrorists used.

General Mulholland's team got to work during the urgent days that followed 9/11. "One of the things we pride ourselves on is the amount of homework we do before we enter an area. We bring in smart guys and we use area studies"—lessons on history, local politics, culture, languages, geography, literature, and other related disciplines—"before going in. We work hard at languages, which is always tough, but it's a window into a culture and how to build a relationship. After 9/11, we had none of that that related to Afghanistan. 9/11 happened, and a few days afterward I was told our group is going to war."

By early October, the team had a strategy and had targeted a local force to be the sharpened end of the spear to start the campaign to unseat the Taliban and eradicate the presence of Al Qaeda from Afghanistan.

With the CIA's help, SF made contact with Uzbek warlord Abdul Dostum. General Dostum, as he was known, had fought against the Russians during the jihad of the 1980s and had been battling the Taliban for years as part of the fractious Northern Alliance, which had a tenuous hold on portions of northern Afghanistan.

The cooperation between General Dostum's ragtag but fierce forces and a small band of SF operators has become the stuff of legends, the fodder for books and Hollywood movies; and it has come to be known as The Horse Soldiers.

This collaboration wasn't smooth, but because of the training of SF soldiers and their commitments to overcoming challenges, they were able to prevail and establish a cooperation that led to stunning victories against an adversary—the Taliban and Al Qaeda—that were heavily armed and highly committed to their cause.

But at first the SF team couldn't get General Dostum to let them into the fight. The SF team had the ability to call in devastating air strikes, but they needed to get close to the action to do so. "Dostum was very worried that any Americans getting killed would result in us pulling out," General Mulholland recalls. "He was very reluctant to have Americans on the front lines, which we needed to help coordinate airstrikes and advise on strategy. It's ultimately all about trust and respect—these people have been fighting all their lives, and now they have a bunch of white guys—infidels—come in; and no matter how good you are, you face a credibility question."

The team worked hard to build the relationship with General Dostum, to show that they respected him and his soldiers, and to try to build that credibility. They insisted repeatedly that they had skin in the game, pointing out the thousands of dead Americans back at home due to the same adversary lurking in the valleys below them now, and they made it clear that they and the U.S. government knew they were going to take casualties. They spent weeks in caves and on the march or on horseback, continuing to insist to General Dostum "that we needed to get into the fight, that we were there for him, not as white saviors, but to fight with him and his forces. When he finally brought them to the front lines, they proved themselves. They had shown General Dostum respect and trust, but you also had to prove yourself capable; you have to prove you can do your job, that you have courage, especially in that warrior culture."

What resulted was a stunning victory that saw the strategic city of Mazar-i-Sharif fall to the Northern Alliance and those small bands of U.S. soldiers on horseback. The fall of Mazar-i-Sharif was critical. It decimated the Taliban and Al Qaeda forces in the region and demonstrated that there was a new dynamic in a country where it has been famously difficult for foreign forces to prevail. Mazar-i-Sharif had a decent airfield, which, once captured, gave the U.S. and its allies the ability to bring in large amounts of forces, equipment, and supplies to fight the rest of the war.

The lessons that these brave soldiers embody in their work can inspire all of us because we can succeed using the same mindset, even if the fate of a new war doesn't rest on our efforts.

Get even a handful of people together for more than a few days, and a culture develops. Give that culture months and years to solidify, and it will naturally create an in-group/out-group mentality, and even cliques within that group. Understanding that, being respectful of it, and trying to work with it—*By, With, Through*—is a much better approach than just bulldozing through with your point of view and style. Your reputation might precede you, but the team you have joined, or the one that you're visiting, or the one that you're prospecting or seeking a relationship with, needs to see your competence;

they need to feel your respect for their norms and their way of doing things. This is what the behavioral scientists were looking for in the 1950s when SF was created; and this is, in part, what CIA recruiters look for in potential new recruits for the Agency. Intellectual curiosity, a respect for others, a problem-solving approach—these are valuable assets when they are natural traits in an individual—especially an individual with incredible physical gifts—but they can also be cultivated. Just like developing an active listening practice, you should develop the kind of cultural flexibility that SF use to win.

Another lesson from General Mulholland's experience revolves around management. Management should always learn from and respect the perspective of those on the ground.

At the start of the Afghan war and Operation Enduring Freedom, a group of Green Berets had made progress developing relationships with members of the Pashtun tribe in the southern areas of Afghanistan. Cultivating the Pashtuns was considered essential because they are the dominant tribe in Afghanistan and the core of the Taliban movement. Breaking off elements of that tribe from the Taliban could create fissures within the organization of Afghanistan's cruel rulers, who—as we saw—were already losing ground in the north due to the collaboration of the Northern Alliance and SF forces. General Mulholland employed a group of Green Berets to cultivate the Pashtun, and there is perhaps no better group to do such work. As discussed earlier, within the SF world, the Green Berets are considered the best in when it comes to collaborating with indigenous forces.

As General Mulholland tells it, "The U.S. government was very focused on bringing to justice any senior Afghan leader who had anything to do with working with Mullah Omar [the leader of the Taliban] or bin Laden. There was a senior Pashtun leader who was working with us now, but he was suspected of leaving the back door open for Mullah Omar to escape from U.S. forces. This Pashtun leader had a big militia that was now cooperating with us, and I had only eighteen or twenty SF guys with him. We were getting pressured by D.C. to bring this guy back and arrest him, but my guys told me it's going to be Mogadishu all over again" (referencing the infamous debacle of "Blackhawk Down'" fame in Somalia in the early '90s). "And if they see us take their leader they'll be coming for us. I had to figure out how to placate the U.S. government while also reaching our objectives. One of my guys on the ground said, 'Let me work this, and I will come up with a solution.' He worked his relationships, and it turned out the guy the U.S. wanted had serious health problems. My guy told him that we know you have health problems, and we also have some questions for you from U.S. leadership. He asked him if he would be willing to get taken to a U.S. ship in the Persian Gulf with top healthcare facilities to get his health issues treated and then answer some questions, and the guy agreed. He wasn't put in the brig after we got our hands on him. He was treated with respect. The interrogators met with him; and when they were done, he returned to his guys. We avoided a bloodbath."

Mulholland had listened to this team on the ground.

Again, there are some clear lessons for leaders of any organization. Leadership might lay out a goal for the company, but if the people in the trenches push back and say it is impossible or will hurt areas of the business, it's incumbent upon leadership to listen. It seems simple, but it's a truth that is all too often ignored by senior corporate leadership. Whether it's hubris or just a lack of respect for the various cultures that develop within any reasonably sized

---

* The Blackhawk Down incident refers to the U.S. military action in October 1993 where the U.S. and a coalition of international partners intervened in Somalia's civil war and as a result saw 18 U.S. deaths and 73 injured in the two-day battle.

organizations, I've seen many examples of corporate leaders laying out strategies that nearly everyone below them groans about.

The U.S. military is a sprawling organization composed of millions of people, and it surely doesn't always manage to pull off the clear managerial dictum of listening to those in the field. But it does, as a philosophy, empower leaders in the field to take action and think independently, which fosters the kind of creative thinking that helped General Mulholland's team avoid a bloodbath and actually grow their relationship with a key, if problematic, ally. This empowerment of independent thinking is also present in how CIA case officers operate, and it comes up over and over again in my conversations with intelligence and military veterans. Several have also pointed out how the Russian military does not operate in this way, but rather features a top-heavy approach to decision-making, which slows down teams in the field and inhibits creative thinking. It's one of the reasons, in the estimation of these sources, that the Russian military—at the time of this writing—has performed so poorly in its ill-advised invasion of Ukraine.

## MANAGEMENT AND ETHICS

Working with and respecting local cultures. Empowering your teams to give feedback, make their own decisions, and act creatively. These are natural segues to a conversation about how leaders from national security and law-enforcement agencies manage their teams and create ethical organizations.

General Stanley McChrystal has a valuable perspective on management and leadership, having been a Green Beret early in his career and then moving up the ranks until he was one of the top leaders in the most powerful military in the world. He points to his initial training as a Green Beret as a foundation of how he came to deal with people with a wide variety of skills and backgrounds throughout his career.

"When I was young, I went into Special Forces, I was a Green Beret, and the training taught you about working with other cultures, how to train guerrillas to get them to work closely with you. We trained in western North Carolina,* with Marines playing the guerrillas, and some of the locals living there played the role of locals in these far-off locations. They received no compensation, but they loved doing it. Some played sympathizers, others were warlords and people siding against the guerrillas. They developed their personalities and they stayed in their roles. What I learned was invaluable in the rest of my career. You're always going to deal with people—they have personalities, things they want; nothing fits an equation."

Remember the Walt Whitman quotation from earlier in this chapter? People are messy, they have multitudes, they don't easily fit into categories and don't always just take orders and start marching, especially when things on the ground look much different than what leadership claims.

"As I got more senior, I learned I was more of an influencer and less of a commander," General McChrystal points out. It's a rather extraordinary remark from someone who was literally the commander of hundreds of thousands of people in Afghanistan. "It's all about influencing people. I have to get you to do what I want you to do, I have to be flexible to make that happen. That training earlier in my career in the SF helped me deal with different cultures and difficult people. In Afghanistan I had forty-six different groups that I was commanding." Because of the famously complex patchwork of Afghan tribes and the dozens of foreign allies who joined the fight with the U.S., General McChrystal couldn't

---

* Known as the Robin Sage exercise.

just command everyone to do his bidding. On the contrary, "you could give almost no direct orders; anything that mattered was done through influence." With a laugh, he reflects on the fact that the lessons learned from his days of SF training proved to be most useful closer to home than in some far-flung location. "It was most useful in dealing with the State Department and CIA; they were on my side, but they had different views and agendas."

When I train teams on how to influence their targets and better communicate as an organization, leaders often convey frustration with their sales reps who come to them with problems that the reps expect them to solve. Some call this "throwing it over the wall."

A common cause of this problem is poor relationship-building. The sales reps have usually done a less-than-stellar job establishing rapport, fostering a dynamic of honesty, and developing other critical details that could help them act creatively to solve problems. But another cause is failing to train the sales reps to understand the perspective of leadership. As General McChrystal notes, "The big problem is the wall. Sometimes people live in different ecosystems, assuming that people on that side have a similar frame of reference to see things the same way." Too often, leadership's priorities and perspective of the market and its challenges are somewhat unclear to those below them. Sales reps end up believing that leadership, viewed as didactic yet sacrosanct, must have a solution to this problem. Management gives orders; the team is expected to execute. It seems that simple. But the team in the field is the one getting direct feedback from clients; and when that feedback on the product or service differs from how leadership views it, a chasm could develop that hurts the bottom line of the company.

"You need to figure out that common frame of reference," as General McChrystal puts it.

John Sipher collaborated with General McChrystal and seems to see things in a similar manner. "Management is about communicating; all people are different, and you need to listen and be very structured about how you listen. You want people under you to hear a lot about how you think and how you process, so they know where you're going and how you want something done, so they don't have to ask all the time. The best-case officers take ownership of the mission, they try to understand what people are doing above and below them so they can think through answers. Good leaders walk their team through their thought process, pushing them to understand what they are trying to accomplish. If they are just coming to the top and looking for answers, they aren't serious players in the organization, they aren't accepting ownership."

And here's a critical insight: Leadership might get upset with underlings asking them to solve their problems, but it could be their own failure. It's essential to train your teams to understand your thinking so they need your guidance less and are empowered to be creative in solving issues. Ideally, a sales rep turns to leadership to say "Hey, I'm facing this challenge, here are a few ways I'm thinking of handling it. What do you think? Am I missing anything?" Then the conversation becomes a brainstorming session between two informed people. The best decisions will get made collaboratively by leaders *and* those in the field together, just like General Mulholland demonstrated by taking in the essential feedback from his team.

Teams are able to avoid throwing problems over the wall if they have a clear sense of the organization's mission and its ethical standards. Recall the story of my early days in corporate security when my CEO shared the anecdote about declining a client's request. The executive team backed up their team in the field and did the right thing in saying no to the client. By communicating well and understanding how we approached our missions, we avoided taking the risky route in Iraq that was ultimately taken by Blackwater contractors, who wound up strung up from a bridge in Fallujah.

The Fallujah incident—or rather how we avoided it—is a great example of clear ethical messaging from leadership. My CEO let us all know our standards and how strongly we felt about them. While the company was in the business of making a profit, that money came second to its ethical standards. We were all expected to adhere to those standards, and I believe that expectation stiffened all our spines and fostered pride in our work. We were even encouraged to convey this story to distinguish our company from the competition, and I saw time and again how this example of ethics and professionalism resonated with my clients.

When talking with a client about executive protection and how we went about it, I let them know that our agents were typically unarmed. This revelation surprised some members of corporate security teams, but I would explain that aside from a few very risky countries we operated in (such as Afghanistan and Iraq), any client request for an armed security detail had to be escalated to our ethics committee, who reviewed the situation and the threat level and would often decline to arm the detail. It was on me to explain to the client that our operators were highly experienced military veterans who usually carried non-lethal weapons (like a collapsible steel rod) and knew very well how to handle physical threats without a gun. We focused on route planning to avoid problems and escape-route awareness to get the principal out of harm's way in case there was an incident. Modifying that Sun Tzu quote from *The Art of War* once again, the best executive protection operator is the one that doesn't fight.

Similarly, we had ethical answers to shipping companies who would ask our advice about arming their crews in pirate-infested waters or whether we would provide an armed detail aboard the ships. We would explain that the better strategy was non-lethal deterrence to keep the pirates off the ship (fire hoses to blast them off, long-range acoustic devices to intimidate and startle the attackers) and building safe rooms for the crew to hide in should that fail. Turning sailors without military training into soldiers was a recipe for disaster; putting contractors on board to kill pirates invited a cascade of crisis-management issues (e.g., employees upset with their company's killing of desperately impoverished people and the media digging in on a juicy story that could make the company look bad).

I was empowered to push back gently on these client requests, and I was armed with solid thinking about why we as an organization, deeply experienced in these matters, advised what could be counter-intuitive strategies. I advocated for these strategies with passion, believing in the mission and standing proud of the ethics and experience that informed them. Clients were impressed. They took our advice. I didn't have to call my manager every time a client wanted an armed detail or to train their crews on how to kill pirates.

I carried a well-defined ethical component to each mission, and the benefits were clear.

Let's dig in more on ethics to understand the ethical code of spies.

## THE ETHICS OF ESPIONAGE

Ethics and espionage? It might be a strange union to wrap your head around. After all, spies are in the business of stealing secrets and persuading agents to betray their countries. But if you scratch below the surface just a bit, you see very clearly that the best CIA case officers strive for moral behavior in an amoral world.

Most of the people drawn to such clandestine work are patriots there to serve the country, not James Bond wannabes. The amped-up adventurers are weeded out in the recruitment process. The ones who are ultimately recruited tend to be decent people who had been raised to never, ever do the things that the Agency is going to train them to do. The Agency provides them with a variety of instruction, rules, and considerations to help guide their actions.

No one can speak to the world of spy ethics like Bob Grenier. One former case officer described Bob to me as "the intellectual's spy," and he certainly has something deeply professorial and erudite about him. But beyond Bob's intellect, it's his unique experience that qualifies him as an expert on the subject of ethics. In addition to years of work in the field as a case officer, Bob was President George W. Bush's designated point person for briefings on intelligence efforts in Iraq during the second Iraq war. He finished his career at the Agency as head of the Counterterrorism Center, overseeing all counterterrorism efforts around the world, and making life-and-death decisions.

Early in Bob's career, he oversaw The Farm and revamped the training curriculum to include ethics instruction. Up until this point in the 1990s, ethics was seen as something an agent either had or didn't have, and ethics were often situational, never a top priority. But a series of Agency mishaps followed by new leadership led to change.

In May 1995, President Bill Clinton appointed former Secretary of Defense John Deutch to lead the CIA. From the Navy, John brought over Nora Slatkin, former assistant secretary, to serve as executive director, a role she held until 1998. Slatkin swore by the military's mantra that "there is nothing that can't be trained"; so when she asked about ethics and was given the "either you have it or you don't" spiel, she moved to make changes. That's when Bob became head of The Farm.

"We had to look at what I saw as the hierarchy of loyalties," Bob recounts. "At the top was adherence to the constitution and the law. At the same time, we instilled the idea of protecting assets, but you also had to put them at risk for the mission. If the priority is keeping your assets safe, it would be at the expense of the mission—and we had to prioritize the mission. That was second. So then the responsibility to protect assets became third, and the responsibility to the Agency was fourth. I wanted to be clear that keeping the asset safe takes priority over the Agency. Laying that all out in very clear hierarchical terms was extremely important, and having stories to support that rationale was also an essential part of the new ethics training. It was less about people doing the wrong thing when they knew the right thing—I was much more concerned about the capacity to do the wrong thing when they thought they were doing the right thing. A case officer might think 'I'm protecting the reputation of the organization'—but we have a job to do, so I don't want that officer prioritizing the wrong things. If we're doing a certain mission authorized by the president and it's lawful and the risk of failure is high, it's not permissible to slow-roll it just because it could embarrass the organization. As long as it's legal, it has to take precedence over the reputation of the organization."

This training helped a new generation of case officers to understand their responsibilities in a world famous for its moral ambiguity.

A training emphasis on storytelling to back up these priorities and to demonstrate what makes them real is important; and, as always, such anecdotes make learning so much easier to digest.

Bob tells a story "where we were operating against an adversary and there were a number of human agents who were rolled up, captured, and some were executed. As we looked back on it, those people were of course taking considerable risks, but it was in the context of advancing vital U.S. national security interests. Still, as we continued to review what had happened, we saw that in some cases there were risks that agents were taking on our behalf that weren't worth it to them. We learned that in those situations, we shouldn't have been running them—they were making only a marginal difference and at considerable expense. One agent I recall spent years in prison. We have to continue to ask ourselves—does the risk to the asset outweigh the success of the operation? Those were the things we started teaching, and we made it very clear what our expectations were in that regard, and we underscored on a more emotional basis what it means when people fail to follow those priorities that we had laid out."

John Sipher notes that "everything we do overseas is illegal; espionage is illegal wherever you go. The U.S. government empowers us with incredible latitude to do things, and you need to understand rules and regulations so you don't go over them." What Sipher is referring to here is that despite the universal illegality of espionage, every government has guidelines about how to navigate this shadowy business—such as "no license to kill." Most emphatically he says that case officers should "only make spies out of people with access to info we can't get in any other way, because we then put people in harm's way."

The need for ethical guidance for case officers is more important than ever as technology rapidly advances. In the past, the Agency often recruited agents to develop a clear understanding of an organization, not just steal its secrets. The end game was to assess who were the potential targets within an organization who were even more high value than the original agent. That recruit would supply the Agency with details about their organizational cohorts—who had a sick child who couldn't get the right healthcare in their country, who was from a less powerful ethnic tribe and was always passed over for a promotion. This information might lead to the next recruit. Much of that work can be done today with electronic intercepts, obviating the need for time-consuming recruitment efforts that put case officers and, in particular, agents at risk.

Bob has written and spoken widely on ethics and espionage, and his thinking translates well to the business world. "For an organization to be truly ethical," he says, "all its members must understand the core values which guide it and the specific ways in which those values are expressed in their daily work. Moreover, that understanding must be broadly accepted and overtly promulgated to empower even the most junior practitioners to proclaim the organization's values, and to hold their superiors accountable for following them."

Recall my former CEO's telling us the story of the moral failure of our competitor, Blackwater. It strengthened our understanding of our organization's ethics. In this case, the CEO did exactly what Bob had moved the entire CIA training apparatus to emphasize— organizational ethics that not only sought to mitigate the risk of bad decisions and behavior, but also empower its practitioners to *advertise* our values and make sales based on them.

What does your organization do to help its team understand its values and mission? Does it give its employees a clear sense of priorities on how to go about reaching their goals? Profitability is at the heart of any business, but what does your sales team know about distinguishing themselves from the competition with their dedication to your values?

I work with a company in the interior design space and they have a commitment to sustainability, which their sales team is passionate about. They make their environmentalism part of their pitch, and it helps them win business. Remember what I noted about how in the marketplace most businesses aren't differentiated, so in this case a product that is more environmentally friendly helps the client to choose them, especially if their own company or end-client has a similar commitment or values.

The sales reps know that when they walk into a pitch it's not the environmental angle that will win them their client. They have been trained in the hierarchy of priorities—they understand that the quality of their product and ability to deliver is the top priority; they know that they must establish a rapport with a variety of vendors working on a big project. But they also know that if they lean on their ethics, if they advertise their company's dedication to a better environmental future without trading off quality of product, it will distinguish them in that crowded marketplace.

Doing the right thing and being a good leader doesn't have to come at the expense of the bottom line. When it's done right, executing on the vision of having a diverse team, focusing on building a business long-term, and growing an organization that is proud of its company's mission and ethics will benefit the company. Government agencies have provided us the model through how they have managed their own success when the stakes aren't just dollars and cents but life and death.

## KEY TAKEAWAYS

So many things go into whether a sale gets made that have nothing to do with how good your product or service actually is. We must be flexible and align ourselves with the culture that we're selling into, being mindful of what is important to that potential client and how they operate. Similarly, good communication is essential if you've moved up the corporate food chain to manage a team, because you then need to get beyond your own ideas and priorities, listen to those in the field, and think about building teams and motivating them for their mission the same way spies do.

1. Use the Atmosphere and Intangibles you pick up from a client to help guide you in your approach. Be sensitive to how an office is decorated, or how your clients interact with you, to discern what is most important to them, what makes them feel comfortable, etc.

2. You can judge a book by its cover! Behavioral science has shown us that we are usually correct in our snap judgments about people, and that should absolutely inform who you approach and how you do it. Just be mindful that people are complex and often contradictory, so don't get stuck on your initial assessment.

3. Look to the world of espionage to get beyond the corporate blind spot of note-taking. Capturing all the details you can about your clients and the culture they are operating in will pay dividends over both the short and long term.

4. Diversity isn't just about skin color and gender. High-performing government teams pull together people with diverse backgrounds to approach problems in novel ways and provide different perspectives on challenges.

5. To empower your team, look to how the CIA has established a hierarchy of ethical standards to guide their decision-making. Understanding the values of your company can help your team to feel proud of how they operate and clarify their mission.

# 4

# SKILLS OF SOCIAL INFLUENCE

*How the FBI and other government agencies
leverage behavioral science to get what they need*

I first joined the corporate-security industry with a British firm with decades of history and offices around the world. This firm was best known as a market leader in the field of kidnap-for-ransom negotiation. Most people are not aware that such a niche industry even exists. Its secretive allure was certainly an attraction for me.

The world of kidnap-for-ransom—or K&R as it's known to those in the know—is a shadowy industry, necessarily secretive and full of highly skilled consultants. The K&R space works collaboratively with another niche corporate sector known as special risk insurance—essentially kidnapping insurance.

Every company or NGO that has its employees traveling or based overseas has a special risk insurance policy, and if they don't it is a kind of negligence. But the details of the policy, and even its existence, are secrets closely held by an organization's leadership, often known only by the CEO and the general counsel. The reason is obvious: organizations don't want to publicize the fact that there is a policy that provides for a substantial ransom to be paid to anyone who kidnaps one of their employees. Such a revelation would motivate bad actors.

When these kidnappings happen, they are kept quiet. The truth is that ransoms are paid every day by companies around the world to get their employees back. At the firm I worked for, the K&R team had a Chinese Wall between its activities and the rest of our company: these cases were that sensitive. We sanitized the cases with letters of the alphabet to keep details secret (instead of using company names or the names of individuals captured); but to give you a sense of how many of these cases there were, in the first year I worked at this firm in the late 2000s we went through the alphabet two and a half times.

I had a bit of experience looking into the world of K&R before I joined this firm. It was a significant reason for my hire.

Working as a stringer for a Singaporean business paper, I managed to secure passage on a Singaporean Coast Guard vessel that patrolled the Strait of Malacca, in particular the dangerous maritime border with Indonesia. At this time in the mid-2000s, pirates from the Indonesian province of Aceh were regularly attacking and taking over boats in the straits, ransoming their crews. Tensions were high in this vital commercial waterway—so narrow at some points that there were just a few miles between Singapore and Indonesia. There were credible threats that Al Qaeda and other Islamic extremists were plotting to blow up a big vessel. If done at one of those narrow chokepoints, it could have brought shipping traffic to a standstill and dealt a serious blow to the global economy.

We saw no pirates on my day on the water, but we did see some ancient-looking Indonesian junks, and the contrast between these 19th-century vessels and the modern military cutter I was on was stark.

As a macabre postscript, the issue of Indonesian pirates was solved in 2004, not long after my reporting trip, when the Indian

Ocean tsunami hit in December 2004. The tsunami hit Aceh particularly hard with waves reportedly a hundred feet tall wiping out buildings and infrastructure and killing approximately 170,000 people, apparently including all the pirates. There hasn't been much piracy in the Strait since then.

My experience reporting on the issue proved valuable to my new employers because we supported a variety of shipping companies who were focused on the problem of piracy off the coast of Somalia.

At that time, the World Bank estimated that such piracy was costing the global economy around $18 billion annually because of rising insurance premiums and increased fuel prices as ships had to take less efficient routes. Countries around the world banded together to create protected corridors for ships to traverse the treacherous waters off the coast of East Africa. But still, ships were being captured and crews were being ransomed; and while the movie *Captain Phillips* was a thrilling true story, having Navy SEAL sharpshooters end a siege was a rarity. Much more common were big payouts for the pirates, and our firm was responsible for dropping parcels with millions of dollars off the coast of Somalia for these pirates so they would free the hostages.

To mitigate the risks, I worked on projects advising shipping companies to take non-lethal measures to protect their ships, crews, and cargoes. These methods included using high-volume acoustic devices to blow out the eardrums of marauders, installing intense fire hoses that could blast water at them, and putting barbed wire around the hulls of the ships to discourage pirates climbing up onto the ship decks, should they get that far.

A big debate in the industry centered around whether or not to have armed guards or crew members onboard. We counseled against such measures. First, it wasn't fair to the crew, most of whom typically had no military experience, or much experience firing a gun at all, to ask them to take up arms for their employers. Most importantly, the mindset of an impoverished Somali pirate who is motivated to keep the crew alive for a potential payoff changes if one of his compatriots is shot and killed. Now, retribution enters the equation.

We successfully counseled our clients to lean into our non-lethal strategies and trust in their high-premium insurance policies. Keep your ships and crews safe, and get them home in case acoustic devices, fire hoses, and barbed wire don't work out.

We held training workshops with clients to prepare them for K&R situations. We would bring in a dozen or so CSOs to run through scenarios and lessons on dealing with such circumstances.

My firm looked for volunteers to audit these workshops and to play certain roles to make them more lifelike. We needed employees to role-play a meddling journalist (not a stretch, considering my recent work), worried family member, and other identities. I raised my hand.

That was how I came to know Gary Noesner and Stephen Romano, both former chief hostage negotiators at the FBI. These incredible men came to be teachers of exceedingly valuable skills that I have used in my career.

The K&R workshops were amazing windows into this little-known world. K&R events are enormously complicated and taxing on any company, and once companies realize this fact, they are inclined to take whatever measures possible to prevent them (short of halting normal business and travel) and to ameliorate them should they occur. The insurance companies are on the same page, with every motivation not to pay out on the policies and to work with their clients to avoid their happening. That's why insurance companies include tens of thousands of dollars in their policies for "subvention funds." Clients use the money to train on how to avoid a K&R situation or to mitigate the downside risks should one still occur.

Once a K&R situation happens, it can quickly go off the rails. That old Tolstoy saying about how each family is dysfunctional in its own way, to roughly paraphrase, always rears its head. Maybe the employee kidnapped is divorced and remarried, and while her current husband is listening to the K&R consultant and adhering to the policy of not talking to the media, the first husband is an attention-seeker and doing multiple interviews. The media noise reaches the kidnappers. Now they see the case as high-profile, and their financial expectations grow. Employees at the company become even more rattled as the crisis appears to spiral out of control. If it's a publicly traded company and word gets out about the kidnapping, it's possible the stock price could be impacted.

The K&R seminars we ran had pearls of wisdom. If you're a hostage, should you try to escape? Think twice, unless you're highly confident about success. Should you fight your attacker? If you're a woman and the event takes place in the developing world, don't fight, because it's all about ransom; but if you're in the developed world, do fight because it's more likely about predation. I learned it was better to be taken by a criminal gang than a terrorist organization, because the former is only interested in money and will keep you safe until they are paid, but the latter have political goals that can result in years-long imprisonment or even death.

We discussed what happens during a K&R event and what these CSOs should be prepared for. The K&R consultants at my firm were typically ex-law enforcement with a sprinkling of former State Department or British Foreign Service members with a good head for negotiation and people management. They tended to work three weeks on, three weeks off, with a bag packed to jump on a plane to any part of the world the moment they were needed.

When an incident arose, one consultant typically deployed to the corporate headquarters for what is known as "hand-holding." Once there, the consultant managed the complex web of stakeholders I alluded to earlier (families, employees, the media, etc.) and helped the company make good decisions with one goal in mind: getting the company's employee(s) home safely.

The other K&R consultant deployed to the crisis site, but not to do the negotiation with the kidnappers. This consultant helped identify a suitable negotiator (if one hadn't already been identified; we would frequently help clients plan ahead for a K&R event by identifying an appropriate negotiator in a hotspot where K&R was a potential issue). The motto was that we were "a coach, not a player." When you think about it, having someone with a posh British accent get on the phone with criminals holding someone hostage might give the criminals the idea to ask for more money than if the person had been someone with a local accent. So the K&R consultant helped identify a local employee, a lawyer, or even a priest, to interface with the kidnappers, all with the K&R consultant and their vast experience and knowledge of the marketplace for payments for people. The consultant was to inform and guide the negotiation. In my years of working in the industry, I wasn't aware of any of our clients being killed or even hurt badly. It was all about the money, and the kidnappers got paid nearly every time.

My reason for sharing with you these details—in addition to hoping you find this stealthy world rather interesting—is to highlight the niche skills such industry players develop. Those same skills, as I will show in this chapter, can help us in our careers and personal lives.

Gary and Steve introduced me to a world of people skills that few ever get to see. These two men have managed hundreds of fraught crisis situations and have access to top-level psychological training. They have a very particular knowledge base.

They worked on high-profile cases like the 1993 Branch Davidian siege in Waco, Texas; the 1996 Montana Freemen siege; and countless other hostage situations. You might be thinking, *Yeah, but that situation in Waco didn't work out so well; are we really learning from the guys that oversaw that?* If you dig deeper into the Branch Davidian siege (the *Waco* series on Netflix, which Gary advised on, and his book *Stalling for Time* are good resources), you'll find that an overly complex web of stakeholders can lead to bad decision-making, and in cases where a siege ended badly it is often because the men with guns weren't listening carefully enough to the crisis negotiators.

One of the philosophies of hostage negotiators, as articulated by Gary, is "Don't get even, get your way." What does this mantra mean? And how do we execute it? Let's look at Gary's and Steve's skills of defusing difficult encounters, spotting deceptive behavior, and negotiation.

## DEFUSING DIFFICULT ENCOUNTERS

The value of defusing difficult encounters is something we can all understand. We all likely agree that each of us could do better, too. It could be anything from a small encounter gone awry with someone in the service industry up to a hostage standoff. Defusion is at the heart of what these FBI professionals do. And defusion skills are applicable to our careers and personal lives.

To some extent, the right mindset and personality are keys. If you spend time with Gary and Steve, you not only note two intelligent people with interesting points of view but also people with the ability to deftly navigate social interactions to avoid friction. These personality traits are what we would look for in the K&R industry when identifying potential negotiators in crises. Having "a slow heartbeat," as you often hear attributed to elite athletes operating under high-pressure situations, is also extremely helpful.

But Dr. Mike Webster will tell you that those traits need not be innate for someone to successfully deal with a hostage situation. We can be *trained*. A Canadian PhD and renowned behavioral psychologist who has for decades trained law enforcement in his home country, as well as FBI agents at Quantico, Dr. Webster is a highly sought-after expert voice on crisis negotiation. He has worked directly on-site at many hostage sieges, including the Branch Davidian siege, as an assistant to the FBI. I believe that if Dr. Webster and Gary had been listened to more carefully, that tragedy in which 76 people were killed (including children) could have been averted.

Dr. Webster has spent untold hours training law-enforcement men and women who might not have the profile as a good crisis negotiator. These public servants often didn't go to college and were drawn to law enforcement as a way to assert their will—tough guys who like telling people what to do. That kind of approach, any seasoned crisis negotiator will tell you, won't get you very far in avoiding loss of life and ending a siege with the least possible bloodshed and destruction.

Dr. Webster molds law-enforcement alphas—who, like their spy counterparts, have to deal with a wide array of humanity and often with people they would not want anything to do with in their personal lives—into law-enforcement professionals with a more sophisticated approach to standoffs. Dr. Webster trains them to find ways to connect with, and seek to understand, hostage-takers in order to defuse a tense situation and avoid violence.

Remember Gary's philosophy of "Don't get even, get your way"? Recalibrate your approach to difficult encounters to this specific mantra. You want to get the best outcome—not necessarily one in which you solely prevail at the expense of the other person. That retribution might feel good in the moment, but during a business negotiation it could lead to an immediate backlash, or to problems that develop over time, or even to an argument with an old friend, which might result in losing that valued relationship.

Learn to avoid taking offense in your business and your life. "You have to be a duck," Gary notes. Let the water roll right off your back if a situation is trending toward the argumentative. Someone might say to Gary, "You could be a real jerk, buddy," and he might reply, "That's what my wife says, but I'd love to learn more about what's bothering you." If he instead argued back, he could be destined for a fight, so he chooses not to provide fuel to the fire.

Easier said than done, right? Especially when tensions are high. We're only human, after all, and who likes to be insulted? But Gary points out: "We're not in the business of winning the argument. You win by getting the person to do what you want. What you want is for them to cooperate, not to become violent or return to violence. Achieving that goal is more important than settling a score." Couldn't the same be said in a business negotiation or an argument with a friend? Even if the stakes are lower, isn't it not so much the threat of violence that you want to defuse, but the destruction of a relationship and all the cascading secondary effects that could follow?

Gary notes that the number-one attribute of a good crisis negotiator, a critically parallel trait to good active listening, is likability. Actually, these traits aren't so much parallel as they are interwoven. Being a great active listener makes you more likable. "Likability is the thing that I've focused on for decades," Gary says, "being a likable, genuine, sincere person. The people you're dealing with will forgive your mistakes because they have a sense of your demeanor and engagement. You don't have to solve people's problems and manipulate them"; but to get a good outcome in a situation you're invested in, it helps enormously to have the other side like you, or at the very least let them dislike you less.

Gary tells a story about his role in the Montana Freemen siege to make his point.

In 1996, a standoff developed between the Montana Freemen and law enforcement. Tensions had, in fact, been developing for years between the government and this group of self-styled "Christian Patriots" who rejected the authority of the federal government and called themselves "sovereign citizens," claiming they were outside the writ of any government. The group engaged in a variety of criminal activities, including forging checks for millions of dollars and conducting mock trials in which death sentences were levied against government officials who offended them.

After years of illegal activity that proved more than the tiny local police department of Jordan, Montana, could handle, the FBI lured away two of the leaders of the group in an undercover operation and arrested them. The hope was that the rest of the group would surrender peacefully after they lost their leaders. But instead, the group seemingly couldn't decide on whether or not to comply with law enforcement. Ultimately, they dug in their heels, leading to the extended standoff that took place. Arrest warrants were issued. With the disastrous Branch Davidian siege of 1993 fresh in their minds, the FBI gave Gary and his team wider remit to use their soft skills to bring the standoff to an end, rather than the hard skills that had gone awry in Waco.

Gary recounts how early in the siege, some angry militia members who were friends of those barricaded came to the site. "They wanted to talk to someone from the FBI, and I was sent to talk to them. I went along with another agent to a bar where we were to meet them. They wouldn't shake our hands; they were angry and demanded to know why the FBI were trying to kill their people. They claimed that there were armored vehicles ready to attack and all sorts of wild things. We said that those vehicles weren't there and we were not doing the things they said we were doing. We offered to take them to the front and show them that they were wrong, and when we did so it defused them. The agent with me read the charges that we were investigating and noted that it was not about their political views. You see, if you're *engaging* with people, it throws them off. When someone is impulsive and argumentative, they are used to getting into a lot of fights, and their approach typically leads to yelling and physical encounters. But if you don't respond in kind, it defuses their need to be aggressive. If someone says to you, 'You're a real asshole!' and you say, 'Oh, well, I do have my faults,' it deflects things. It's not about winning the argument. Those militia guys ultimately went home, their sails deflated, because they were spoiling for a fight and instead we told them that anything they wanted, we were open to it, we were open to showing them what was really going on."

After an 81-day standoff, the Freemen ultimately surrendered peacefully to Gary and his colleagues from the FBI.

There are a number of practical lessons we can learn from what Gary shared about the Montana Freemen siege, as well as other aspects of his and Steve's career in the FBI.

When Gary sat down at the bar with the angry, aggrieved militia members, he immediately invited them to tell him what was wrong, what was on their mind. As they did so, Gary listened carefully, giving these guys his full attention, despite knowing they were wrong about the facts and surely feeling a compulsion to correct them. But he didn't give in to the urge to argue with the militia members; he let them vent.

Venting is the first place to start when you're trying to defuse someone's anger. Let's say you're a manager on a sales team and suddenly a member of your team, let's call him Tim, bursts into your office. Tim is angry because a new prospect has been assigned to another team member, Jessica, and he is ranting about why this was unfair and how he should have gotten the chance to develop that new prospect.

Your first reaction is to rise to Tim's anger, because you feel he's way off base. Tim has blown the last two prospects that you fed him, and his pitch is not as good as Jessica's. He is also consistently the last team member to arrive to the office and the first one to leave, and his attitude and commitment to his job seem to be lacking in general. So right now you want to shut Tim down, interrupt him, tell him the facts as you see it. You're a busy person, and you don't have time for Tim's nonsense.

But at the moment, you still need Tim. Your team is short-staffed, and he does a decent job on account management with a fairly small book of business. You're working with Human Resources to get new talent on the team, but having a massive blow-up with Tim now could result in his quitting or having to fire him. That's not going to help anyone.

So you sit patiently as Tim rants and skews the facts about the situation; you're letting him vent and fully unburden himself. You don't interrupt him. You don't contradict him. You don't add more fuel to his fire.

Consider *emotional labeling* as a good next step, continuing to keep in mind that it is not about winning an argument, but rather defusing this encounter. You might say to Tim, "It sounds like you're angry that you're not getting more of a chance at developing new business." Labeling Tim's emotions lets him know that you've heard him and respect him enough to *carefully* listen. It gives Tim a chance to correct any false impressions you might have after you've articulated them.

Even if you mislabel someone's emotions, it could have positive consequences. If Tim now says "Yes, I'm upset that I never get a chance at new business at this company. But I'm also pissed because Jessica is always boxing me out with you and getting you to favor her over me."

So now you know that Tim isn't just angry about not getting enough chances at new business (which isn't true, in your estimation, but that *does not matter* at the moment; all that does matter is reducing Tim's anger level so you can have a more reasonable conversation). He also has interpersonal issues with Jessica. We can also see that *tendency to correct* (see Chapter 2) at work once again in these situations, because someone who has had their emotions mislabeled will surely not let that stand: they will correct your impression and thus your communications and the issue will be further clarified.

Your next move is to validate Tim's feelings, even though you don't agree. "I get why you could feel that you're not getting enough chances at new business and how it seems that Jessica is getting more of those chances."

All this time, you're sitting behind your desk and Tim is standing just in front of the closed door of your office. Now that he's done ranting and you've validated his feelings, you invite Tim to sit down and speak with you further. If Tim refuses, you don't stand up to have the rest of the conversation; that will raise the tension in the room. But in this case, Tim feels a bit deflated after he has fully vented, so he accepts the offer to sit down at your desk.

Your next move is to use projection questions to get Tim to feel like a stakeholder in solving this problem. Here are some examples of good projection questions:

- Can you tell me how you see the problem?
- What are your concerns?
- What would a successful outcome look like?
- What are your priorities?

Inviting Tim to be a stakeholder in solving the conflict, not just ranting at you, provides you with the opportunity to continue to exhaust Tim's anger. What often happens as encounters like this play out is that the person arrives at their own unreasonableness and calms down of their own accord, often feeling a little abashed. With Tim, you use a variation of the previous projection questions: "How in your view do we solve this problem, Tim?" Tim replies, "You fire that conniving jerk Jessica and start giving me my fair share of new business opportunities."

Perhaps Tim remains defiant after this outburst of an answer. But he might also realize how unreasonable he's being when he articulates such a demand. That could offer a chance to deflate his anger further and bring him back to a calmer state, where you can talk to him about his career. In such encounters, people are often upset simply about their own behavior and how it has impacted their job and life. If you let them come to that epiphany themselves, rather than rub their faces in it, they can more efficiently digest their situation and move on.

Steve Romano counsels people in these situations to remember that "in all personal interactions, people need to be allowed to save face and maintain some level of dignity." You feel angry that an underperformer like Tim has the nerve to challenge your leadership of the team and attack a colleague who you know has strongly outperformed him. You badly want to say to him, "Tim, it's pretty unbelievable that you storm into my office angry about not getting a new account when you've blown the last two prospects we gave to you. And you have the gall to suggest that we fire Jessica, who is one of the top performers on the team. Stop focusing on Jessica and start pulling your own weight. You might start by not being the last one into the office every day." It would surely feel good to put Tim in his place, but where will that get you? It will lead to a much-needed team member feeling even more aggrieved and maybe even walking out on the job. Remember Gary's quote "Don't get even, get your way."

This is hard stuff, but it is worth it. Let's say Tim has taken a deep breath after his outburst and now appears calm. The hardest part might be the next step: thanking him. But it is worth doing if you're looking at the big picture. If you've settled Tim down and gotten him to be a partner in creating a path forward, thanking him for sharing his feelings with you might feel in direct contradiction with your emotions, but it will further disarm Tim and later he will likely reflect on his respect for you and how you handled the situation.

But if you have tried all these things and Tim hasn't adjusted his tone, taken a seat, or in any way shown that he can be a productive stakeholder in fixing the issue, you should call a time-out. Hold your nose and thank Tim for sharing his thoughts with you and tell him you'd like to think things over and talk later that day or tomorrow.

Gary's memoir is called *Stalling for Time*, and there is a reason why a successful end to a siege like the one with the Montana Freemen took 81 days. Hot situations sometimes simply need real time to cool off.

Remember what Gary said about being a duck with water flowing off your back? These confrontations feel really intense at the moment; we're being challenged, our adrenalin races, we want to protect ourselves and vanquish the person challenging us, physically or otherwise. The smart negotiator in a tense situation is thinking about the overall outcome of things and not the mini-battle in front of them.

It's important to remember something that former FBI agent Joe Navarro stresses: *emotion always trumps cognition*. How many times have you been in an argument with someone, and an hour afterward, you think to yourself, "Dammit, I wish I had said XYZ!"

Or "I wish I hadn't said ABC!" You didn't think of that in the moment because your cognition was overwhelmed by emotion. Your approach to the early stage of someone's anger—to let that person vent—not only offers that person a chance to exhaust themselves, but also, if you train yourself not to interrupt and escalate, allows you the chance to calm down your own emotional state and warm up your cognition. You will avoid decisions that might feel good emotionally in the moment but that will hurt you rationally as the dust settles.

One of the other methods used by the FBI and other law-enforcement professionals involves what's known at the Bureau as "skills of social influence." Human beings are deeply influenced by their surroundings and what other people are doing within those surroundings. So if someone is angry and approaches you while talking loudly and quickly, your task is to avoid responding in kind, and thereby change the environment.

Force yourself to speak at a slower and quieter pace. In time, and if you stick with it, that person will revert to the social mean that you're insisting on. FBI crisis negotiators do this all the time when dealing with someone who has taken people hostage. It's almost a cliché from a movie or TV show, the cool negotiator behind Ray-Ban shades, leaning up against a cop car with armed men scrambling around him to take up positions, speaking calmly to the crazy criminal holding women and children at gunpoint. But it's true, and it works. Try it in a social setting with someone even when it's not an argument, maybe they're just a little too loud and animated, and watch that person quickly revert to the social baseline you're establishing with your slower and quieter speaking voice.

Crisis negotiators independently all relate similar anecdotes regarding post-siege interviews with hostage-takers. When asked why they agreed to come out and end the siege, hostage-takers almost never point to any particular concession made to them or any goal achieved. They point to the crisis negotiator—who has calmed them, mirrored them verbally, labeled their emotions, etc. They say that the crisis negotiator understood them, listened to them. Gary has heard, "It's not what you said, but how you said it."

Remember how difficult it is to listen to every word someone is saying to you and how we tend to pick up the gist as we gather other details from the person (body language, tone of voice)? That's what these hostage-takers are experiencing—they are feeling heard, they have been influenced by the baseline that the negotiator has steadfastly insisted on, and they are responding to that negotiator's disciplined focus on being likable.

Who in the sales world hasn't faced an angry client? Whether the client is upset about your company not providing what you sold them, or not providing it to a standard they expected, or they are annoyed about your fees, even the best salespeople encounter a client upset about something and directing their anger at you. Having these strategies at your fingertips will preserve—and potentially grow—relationships. Let's talk a bit more about these types of encounters and review some other ways to resolve them.

Tzviel "BK" Blankchtein advises on difficult encounters that might involve violence, and he advises businesses and law enforcement on how to de-escalate these situations or recognize the potential for bloodshed and so then prepare for it. A veteran of the Israeli Defense Forces on its infantry reconnaissance team, BK provides clear thoughts on dealing with hostile individuals who can be useful to any of us navigating everyday life while also having relevance to business settings.

BK advises a simple methodology when dealing with someone who seems potentially hostile—Recognize, Address, and

Protect (RAP). After recognizing that you're dealing with some-one hostile, his suggestions on addressing the grievance of the angry person aren't all that different from how the FBI addresses hostage-takers. He trains people to try to understand why the person is angry and to ask people what's on their mind, which shows them a degree of respect and encourages them to vent. BK suggests separating angry people into two categories: 1) Nice peo-ple who could be acting like assholes but, if treated with the right level of respect and understanding, will ultimately comply with well-utilized de-escalation strategies. And 2) Difficult people who seem likely to have these interactions regularly and seem to have the potential to turn violent. He describes trying to distinguish between people who are rude and those who are threatening, calling it "the difference between Fuck You and Fuck This."

This distinction is important. If the person is angry about the situation they are in (Fuck This), it is not specifically about you, though you could potentially be contributing to it. In those cases, you have a chance to de-escalate because you can work with the person on the situation (This). But if they are angry specifically with you (Fuck You), that raises the stakes. BK advises many health-care providers and notes that "people in healthcare who are trying to enforce the wearing of masks have faced people upset about the rules for wearing masks, and one of the first things to do when dealing with such people is to give them a logical explanation about why you are asking them to do what you want them to do, what the rules are, and try to find a way for it to resonate with the person. If the logical explanation about the rules doesn't work, I tell people to provide the angry person with some alternatives: they can wear a bandanna, wait in a different area, or schedule a different time, for example." After a while, if you speak patiently to such a person, and use those FBI strategies about maintaining a calm voice and slower pace, things tend to calm down. As Gary notes, "It's hard to sustain anger when someone is showing that they're listening." Interestingly, BK notes that if you successfully "de-escalate, you have often created an ally" out of someone who was just a few moments ago an adversary. It's a surprising turnabout. But someone who is irate about something is often relieved to deescalate, and if they have been mollified by someone who has tried to understand their concerns and shown them respect, then that sense of relief often manifests itself in a kind of kinship for the person they were just battling.

BK also has experience in working with law enforcement on gang violence. One of the simple strategies he advises has relevance to anyone dealing with an angry person in a group setting: try to get that person away from the group and deal with them one on one. He notes that in gang scenarios, individuals "are usually trying to look tough in front of their peers; but when you separate them from their peers, they start to comply." A subtle form of this happens sometimes in business settings where you have an arrogant client or prospect trying to score points with colleagues by looking clever and taking apart you or your sales pitch. Try not to take the bait. See if you can speak with that person on the sideline. More often than not, they will strike a different tone when it's just the two of you. Hopefully you can build that relationship from there and turn them into an ally.

Difficult encounters don't always involve raised voices and angry accusations. An anecdote from my journalism days has corollaries for our divisive times.

After working on it for months, I finally scored an interview with Mahathir Mohamad, the former prime minister of Malaysia. One of the most significant figures in the history of the Southeast Asia in the late 20th and early 21st centuries,

Mahathir was still arguably the most influential political leader in Malaysia in the mid-2000s despite being out of office and at an advanced age.

Mahathir had achieved a lot in his decades-long career in politics. He oversaw economic growth that led to rising living standards for millions of Malaysians, and he mostly kept the lid on racial strife in his multi-ethnic country.

But he also courted international controversy, with no better example than his response to the Asian Financial Crisis in the late '90s. A contagion swept through the "Asian Tiger" economies, which had recently experienced spectacular growth. Now they were plagued by systemic issues, such as over-building. Mahathir accused international financiers of being behind his country's economic woes and made antisemitic remarks about them, in particular George Soros. Having worked for a Soros initiative while overseas and having spent time with George in China, I was and still remain a huge admirer of what Mr. Soros has achieved by putting his money to good work with his Open Society initiatives. Add to that the fact that I am Jewish myself, and Mahathir's remarks were deeply offensive. Plus, as a journalist who had traveled around Malaysia, I had witnessed the over-building that was symptomatic of the irrational exuberance that had led to the financial bubble bursting. I knew that Mahathir was engaged in a tradition of Jewish scapegoating, one that has been around for hundreds of years, which I found loathsome. Only a few weeks before meeting Mahathir, I was on a sleepy island off Malacca where I stumbled upon a derelict golf course and shuttered resort that the jungle was taking over. In the story I wrote about the experience, I noted that at that time Malaysia had more golf courses per capita than any other country in the world. I'm pretty sure that Mr. Soros had nothing to do with such bad economic planning, but he made a good target for a demagogic leader looking to pass the buck and avoid responsibility.

I met the former prime minister at his grandiose offices on the outskirts of the capital, Kuala Lumpur. He greeted me politely, wearing his trademark songkok hat, and then calmly and patiently answered my questions about international affairs. Some of his remarks were deeply offensive to me. Memories of the second Intifada that had roiled the Middle East were still fresh, and he went on at great length about how the Palestinians had every right to use suicide bombers to attack Israeli civilians. He later went on to defend Iran and how the country had a right to develop a nuclear weapon.

These views were anathema to me. But I was there in my capacity as a journalist; it wasn't my job to try to convince him that his views were morally abhorrent, or to even share my point of view at all. If he said something that I knew was factually incorrect, I politely challenged that; but I wasn't there to debate him.

We ended the discussion and respectfully parted ways. My editors were deeply pleased with the interview, as was his press team, when it ran in *The Far Eastern Economic Review*. This difficult encounter was defused with professionalism (and taking some deep breaths), and that is something we should all keep in mind in the polarizing political times we live in.

We're living in an age of intense political division. As a salesperson, you might be meeting with someone who expresses a political view that you find repugnant. It's not your job to debate this person, to convert them, or to refute their views. Take a breath and change the subject. If your target continues to push the issue, say something like, "I'd rather leave politics out of the conversation, if you don't mind," and then quickly bring something else up.

## NEGOTIATIONS

In many ways, we're already talking about negotiations. Every difficult encounter is a negotiation over how to resolve that particular impasse. So take those elements of dealing with people who are upset about something—certainly not uncommon in a business negotiation—and let's add some other lessons from the world of the FBI and other law-enforcement agencies.

Dr. Webster used a simple illustration to describe a way to think about a crisis negotiation, which we'll see has relevance to business and everyday life as well. He described types of negotiations as falling along a horizontal line with a vertical notch at either end and one in the middle. The far left-hand vertical notch is labeled "instrumentally motivated"; the middle notch is labeled "expressively motivated"; and then the notch on the far right is labeled "high risk."

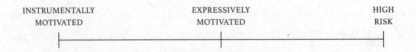

"Instrumentally motivated" is the most common negotiation. The other side is out for a tangible goal, you have yours as well, and how you get there is up to you. In a crisis situation, it might mean that the hostage-takers want compatriots released from jail. In a business situation, it could be a private equity firm buying out a company founder who is trying to get the maximum return for the business she built.

"Expressively motivated" involves a counterpart who is motivated by emotional needs. That means someone who has taken hostages because they are angry that their spouse is leaving them, or that they lost their job, or that a political party they hate has taken power and they want to be paid attention to so they can complain about these things. Sticking with the business example of a company owner negotiating with a private equity firm, it could be a patriarch selling a business that has been in his family for several generations. He is already a wealthy man, so it's less about the ultimate selling price, but none of his children wants to run the firm, and his wife wants him to retire and travel the world. The patriarch is emotionally attached to the company, wants to protect its employees, and is uneasy. He wants to feel that the private equity firm buying his company will look out for his employees and the legacy he has built more than anything.

"High risk" negotiations involve someone unreasonable, who isn't giving the other side a chance to understand them or help them reach a common goal. When law enforcement faces this kind of situation, it typically involves an individual who isn't taking hostages to achieve a goal ("release my comrades") or to be understood ("I'm upset because my spouse doesn't love me anymore"), but someone who seems focused on violence and probably seems scary. They will simply shut down law-enforcement attempts to engage and swear at them and make awful threats of violence, ones that might be particularly credible if that person has a track record of violence or has committed such acts already in this particular siege. The business corollary here is a client who demands that you cut your price to something where you would lose money servicing them or is treating you with hostility.

For the instrumentally motivated, you employ many of the strategies we have been going over. A crisis negotiator would try to establish a working alliance, build rapport with that individual, calm them down with skills of social influence if they are upset, listen deeply to what they want, and start to find areas where you might be able to meet some of their demands as you look to get them to meet yours. In the business world, hopefully you have already established a working alliance with your counterpart, perhaps through months or years of getting to know each other. You can smartly employ tactics like elicitation and active listening to collect information and signal respect, both of which should facilitate a good outcome.

For the expressively motivated, the crisis negotiator wants to simply listen and understand and really use the tools of active listening and emotional labeling. The crisis negotiator will let the person vent, verbally mirror that person, and hopefully lead to the outcome that they see so often: the hostage-taker ending the siege because they felt understood and seen by the crisis negotiator. In the business world, the family patriarch concerned with his legacy and the employees he's worked with for years could be appeased with assurances about keeping the business's name, guarantees for employment of certain employees for a period of time, etc.

One of the tactics that crisis negotiators use is to flag the consequences of not reaching an agreement. Dr. Webster reports that he and Gary were trying to use this consequence labeling with David Koresh during their work on the Branch Davidian siege. Dr. Webster describes Koresh's motivations as "an expressive situation, he felt he had to do what he was doing. But the incident commander was treating it as if it were an instrumental situation, which is why it blew up. If you were listening carefully to what Koresh was saying and you established a solid working relationship with him, at some point you could say, 'I hate to think about what would happen if we don't get to an agreement.'" But because everyone in law enforcement wasn't on the same page with a common strategy to end the siege, it resulted in tragedy.

Citing consequences to advance a negotiation is particularly useful in business settings. If there is an impasse or hesitation from the other side, saying something like, "I'd hate to think that all the good things we could be bringing to your company could fall by the wayside if we don't figure this out," could certainly be appropriate. If the negotiation is far enough along for that to be something germane, it will likely resonate. Never lose sight of the fact that you should have conviction about what you're selling—the client is not doing you a favor. Let them worry about what they will lose out on if they don't come to an agreement with you.

High-risk negotiations are a different matter entirely. If a crisis negotiator is dealing with someone with a history of violence, they have a responsibility to keep that front of mind. If the hostage-taker is not making reasonable demands and is threatening to harm others, a crisis negotiator has to consider using tactical forces to storm the site and end the siege, despite the risks involved. In business, sometimes calculations are made to continue with a client at a loss because the client is a prestigious name, there's a chance the relationship will return to profitability in the near future, or other sound reasons. But no company is obliged to be bullied by a client into taking a loss, which can be dispiriting for a team in addition to hurting the bottom line. No one in business either should be forced to work with, or sell to, a disrespectful client. In both these cases, there's a business-world version of sending in the tactical team: simply walking away from the client. Politely end the negotiation and walk away. Sometimes the other side is bluffing or simply overplaying their hand, and they wind up coming back to you—a valued service provider—hat in hand and ready to take a much more reasonable position.


Ultimately, reframing your thoughts on negotiation to make it less of a zero-sum game—I win, you lose—will result in better outcomes and better relationships. Thinking about negotiation as problem-solving and not a contest, while employing some of the strategies we've just discussed, will put you on a path to success.

Start negotiations with small things that you can get your counterpart to agree on. Let's say there is a hostage siege at a bank. The siege started around six hours ago, and by now everyone inside must be hungry, despite the tension. The negotiator makes an offer to deliver the hostage-taker's favorite food for everyone inside, but in return would they consider sending out a few of the women and children? That is an easy concession to make, and it starts to build momentum on cooperation.

Dr. Webster suggests getting the other side *in the habit* of cooperating with you. He advises to "make it easy for the opposition to agree with you at the same time you make it difficult for them to disagree. Making it easy to agree requires maintaining a problem-solving negotiation approach, while making it difficult to disagree requires an exercise of your force."

Dr. Webster points to a siege situation in 1995 between the Ts'peten Sundancers and the Royal Canadian Mounted Police (RCMP) at Gustafsen Lake, British Columbia, which resulted in a fundamental shift in how Canadian law enforcement approached armed standoffs. Before the successful de-escalation of this siege, the strategy of the RCMP was to *try* to talk to the other side, but if that didn't quickly bear fruit they would mount an armed response. Since the successful resolution of "the situation at Gus Lake," the "easy to agree, hard to disagree" approach has ascended.

The Gustafsen Lake standoff, as it is known, was essentially a land dispute with many volatile elements. An indigenous group with a claim to the land, which is known as Ts'peten in the Shuswap language, felt that their religion was under attack; ranchers with claim to the land felt that they were being pushed out. When the indigenous group built an encampment in 1995 and barricaded themselves while brandishing arms, things escalated and soon hundreds of Canadian law-enforcement agents were on the scene.

An academic paper on the siege notes that "Police tactical presence at Gustafsen Lake was designed to bring inhabitants of the encampment to their senses, not to their knees. Force was used to educate, since inhabitants in the encampment refused to reach agreement because they were convinced they could win, and the reasoned exercise of force gave them an opportunity to discover the consequences of no agreement." So while the tactical forces arrayed around those barricaded on the site were seen as provocative and threatening, their presence was more about credible consequences if an agreement wasn't reached rather than intimidation. It was all about how the RCMP used, or rather didn't use, their forces, while keeping them clearly visible.

Dr. Webster explains that humiliating the opposition or attempting to bludgeon or bully them into submission in a negotiation can backfire. "Face-saving is at the heart of the negotiation process. It is difficult for the opposition to agree with you when they are concerned with how that agreement will make them look to others." The indigenous group on the contested land in Canada felt that they were protecting their religion and their dignity, and they seemed to be prepared to shed blood if necessary, so threats of force were unlikely to bring the standoff to a peaceful end.

Instead, the RCMP took their time in dealing with the situation (remember "stalling for time"?). Not rushing things, especially when emotions are high, is a good policy when it comes to bringing negotiations to a positive end. That goes for business negotiations as much as for armed standoffs. Applying a degree of patience is almost always a good strategy.

The RCMP broke the negotiations down into small points to create a problem-solving negotiation that built momentum on cooperation. They started with a commitment to a cease-fire, moving into smaller details about food and logistics, and then taking on some of the thornier issues that were at the heart of the standoff. The academic paper on the events at Gus Lake noted that "The RCMP relied on the human tendency to infer personal characteristics like attitudes and beliefs from observing our own actions. If the inhabitants of the encampment observed themselves agreeing with the RCMP, even on smaller issues, they would be more likely to view themselves as able to agree with the RCMP on larger issues."

This is a critical point. A negotiation built on solving small issues point by point can build momentum toward a larger agreement. Dr. Webster observes that "human beings feel inconsistent when they commit themselves to something and then turn themselves on it. Get someone to commit themselves to something small, and then get them to come back to things larger each time." Through this process, rapport is built, trust is established, and barriers between the two sides start to come down. There are virtues of give-and-take that don't exist in a zero-sum game.

Nevertheless, your negotiating partner might not have gotten the memo on this enlightened approach to negotiation. Their attempts at the zero-sum game might lead them to aggressively press their agenda. Dr. Webster urges caution. Don't respond in kind to the other side's bullying tactics. "Counterattacking with an offensive action is counterproductive," Dr. Webster explains. "It is provocative and will result in reactance and hardened resistance. Simply neutralizing the opposition's attack without striking back is a more effective use of force. Such neutral use of force is more likely to bring the opposition to their senses and return them to the negotiating table."

He goes further to say that "Several thousand years ago, the great military strategist Sun Tzu stated, 'The best general is the one who never fights.' Restating him to suit our purpose, we might say,

'The best crisis manager is the one who never assaults.'" Again, the applications for business are clear: try to be the negotiator in the sales world who is never provocative, who never attacks, but calmly allude to the negative consequences of not reaching an agreement.

At the heart of every good negotiator is an understanding of empathy. We've seen case officers using empathy to build relationships with potential agents, but it's also essential in negotiations.

The FBI considers empathy in hostage cases as simply the identification or understanding of the hostage-taker's situation, feelings, and motives. This approach should be used by anyone engaged in a negotiation of any sort. Start with the question of what your counterpart's motivation is in this negotiation. Check in with your counterpart on that goal as the negotiation continues. Keeping tabs on the other side's goal motivation, mindset, and emotions will allow you to plot your next moves. Applying tactical empathy allows you to influence emotions based on an understanding of your counterpart's goals, which you will have thought about carefully. Even if the negotiation fails, you can walk away with a relationship intact for future benefit.

Steve Romano calls empathy "the WD-40 of communication"— it will lubricate the gears, help move things along. Dr. Webster notes that emotion-labeling should be an essential ingredient of an empathetic approach. Empathy is not a trick. It doesn't fool your counterpart into thinking you're an ally because you seem to have understood where they are coming from. Rather, we are conditioned toward empathy. "There is nothing in the brain that makes empathy happen," Dr. Webster says. "If I feel that someone understands me deeply, it doesn't do something specific in my brain. It causes me to think based on my *social development* [italics added for emphasis] through the years—this person understands me. People who understand me are people who will be of service to me, are more enjoyable to be around, etc. It's more learning-based than physiological-based. I like being with people who listen to me, who seem to understand me." Empathetic people are more inclined to treat others as they've been treated, to be fair, and they seek to understand motivations and consider how the other feels about the outcome you're negotiating.

## MEETINGS, INTERVIEWS, AND PITCHES

One-on-one conversation is a bedrock social interaction. But the context in which this interaction takes place varies widely. Let's reframe how you might approach this fundamental human interaction by exploring some different contexts.

Different contexts require distinct approaches in winning people over and influencing them, as we saw in the section on Atmosphere and Intangibles. We'll analyze how military interrogators and FBI counterintelligence agents do their job, and perhaps season it with some journalism experience as well.

Think of a military interrogator. You are probably envisioning some tense scene out of a movie: A stark room with just a table and a metal chair, a detainee, perhaps shackled, likely someone high-ranking—a deeply informed member of the other military, who looks either scared or defiant. The interrogator pounds the table and demands to know the plan of attack. The stakes are high and the attack is imminent.

The real world of military interrogation is quite different.

While the U.S. military might sometimes get its hands on a high-level member of the enemy forces, more often it's a low-level individual who is captured. This person might not know much about battle plans or have detailed knowledge about his side's capabilities. But intelligence collection is about creating a mosaic of information and then gleaning insights from it.

Let's say that the military has captured a truck driver bringing supplies to the enemy's front lines. What's a truck driver going to be able to tell the U.S. military? Quite a bit, potentially. But first let's talk about how the interrogator is going to behave and handle the detainee.

The course of interrogation will be driven in part by how the detainee acts. If we assume that the truck driver is somewhat scared to be in enemy hands and doesn't have counter-interrogation training, we can assume that our interrogator is going to put the detainee at ease. General McChrystal notes: "At the end of the day, interrogation is sales. The best interrogators are salespeople: they establish themselves as human beings and establish rapport; then you start to explore what it is that this individual wants or fears."

Maybe the interrogator walks in with a cold drink for the truck-driver detainee and has a smile and easy manner. The interrogator wants to put the detainee at ease and get them to relax, not bully or threaten them into submission. The interrogator isn't trying to get the detainee to admit something as much as they are trying to get the detainee to simply open up about what they have seen or know about what's going on with the enemy. As Adam,* the military interrogator we met in Chapter 2, notes, "I don't need to prove they're guilty; I'm not interested in a sweaty brow, etc. I want them to continue to talk to me; I want to build a rapport so that they naturally share information with me."

After putting the detainee at ease and trying to establish basic rapport, the interrogator is going to ask about how the enemy troops react when their truck arrives with supplies. Are the enemy soldiers very happy to see them and crowd around the truck, eager to help get the supplies out and utilize them? That is helpful to learn and could tell the military that the enemy is short on supplies or that the logistics bringing them are complicated or otherwise troubled, which has implications about the enemy capabilities and their morale. If the detainee says that their arrival is barely noted, that points to the enemy being well-stocked and supply lines running smoothly.

Did the truck driver have a full tank of gas for the drive to the front line, or do they have gas canisters in the back of the truck or have to stop many times to get fuel in villages along the way? If they're taking up precious space in the truck for canisters or stopping constantly to forage for fuel, that again points to logistics problems.

The interrogator does not scare the detainee. They just talk to them about their job, their basic observations of the world he sees. The interrogator gets the detainee to talk by being easy to talk to and *calm*.

And the interrogator has a plan going into the interrogation. The interrogator knows this person is not going to have critical battlefield intelligence, but they will potentially have a few pieces of small intel that can be very helpful, so the plan will focus on that.

An FBI counterintelligence agent has a different approach going into an interview. Let's say the case she is working involves someone or multiple people leaking sensitive U.S. military information to an adversary. She needs to figure out who is behind these damaging leaks, and the people involved are likely extremely savvy about the system and will not easily reveal what they know. The person she has in the interview room could be totally innocent or just a really good liar. Our FBI agent needs to deploy a canny strategy to figure out which is true.

She will not go out of her way to make her interrogation subject feel comfortable, like our military interrogator with his detainee. She wants to keep her interview subject off-balance, see if they get tripped up or if they keep their story straight. She is going to ask questions with answers she already knows to see if the subject is being truthful. She is going to circle back to questions she has already asked, perhaps subtly phrasing them differently to see if they contradict or undermine previous answers. Crucially, she is going to use her body-language training—which we will go over—to look for deception or soothing behaviors, little pieces of body language we all engage in to calm ourselves down. She'll note those moments and the questions that elicited them to compile a report on the subject's truthfulness.

Context. It changes effective conversation strategy. And training and planning make crucial differences in these conversations. Let's discuss ways you can use similar thinking to gain an edge in business and everyday conversations, and we're going to incorporate how body language plays a big role in evaluating your counterpart.

How you prepare and conduct yourself in a client pitch versus a job or board interview, versus an information-gathering conversation with a friend, has layers of subtlety and distinction.

The first step is preparation. Frankly, I hope you prepare well for any job or board interview you have. You've done your homework on the company's mission, its history, its recent marketplace news, and perhaps what sites like Glassdoor can tell you about the work environment (though these sites can be highly biased, incorporating mostly the notes of aggrieved former employees, I still say it's valuable intelligence).

But have you gathered intel on the person interviewing you, to whom you will pitch your product or service? Hopefully you have looked up that person on LinkedIn—and, better yet, gone deep on their profile and tried to put together a picture of who that person is and how you might click with them.

LinkedIn has become a huge resource for anyone in the business world. While you still find people with very basic profiles, most of us have filled out our profiles with recommendations from others, school affiliations, boards we might sit on, and even charities we support. The résumé of places where a person worked, in what roles, in what cities they were based are extremely helpful in developing a character study of that person. The mutual connections we might share are obviously helpful. But think about the little details—what kind of profile photograph do they feature—and what about the banner image behind their photo? Let's dig into these details.

Let's say you're interviewing for a job with the company CEO, the person who might be your boss, and you want to figure out what will give you a chance to build rapport and connect. You're also going to evaluate the chief to figure out if you'll be happy working for them, and if you can learn from them and grow your career.

The CEO's LinkedIn profile shows them in a suit with only a slight smile. The background behind their photo is blank—they haven't even personalized this image. You want to start at the CEO's beginning, so you scroll down to education. The chief lists a public high school in the Midwest, and you can see from the dates there that this CEO is about fifteen years older than you. After high school, they went to a well-regarded state school and studied business. Right after graduation, they went to graduate school, this time to an Ivy League school, and studied accounting.

The professional-history section shows someone who stays at a company for at least five years, with only a few job changes in a career of a little over two decades. All the jobs have been in Boston, where the CEO has worked since graduate school. The chief's recommendations feature several people saying some variation of the same thing: *hard worker, extremely focused, intelligent, loyal, dependable.* You notice several mutual connections, but, as is common with LinkedIn, only one connection of yours is someone you feel you can reach out to for information on this person.

You contact your source, who reinforces what you've discovered from the CEO's LinkedIn profile. This executive is a serious, driven professional who expects a lot from the team. This chief is not a particularly fun boss, and drives the team hard, but is known as fiercely loyal to the team, sometimes engaging in pitched corporate battles on their behalf, and your source tells you that she learned a lot from this CEO and grew personally and professionally working on their team. You learn from your source—after asking because you saw the board affiliation on the chief's LinkedIn profile—that this person is dedicated to cancer research, having lost a father early in life to leukemia. The chief runs a half-marathon every year to raise money for research, and apparently loves it when the team joins in.

How has that impacted your preparation? Maybe you're someone who has thrived in fun, collegial environments in the past, and you're a bit worried that this CEO might be a martinet. But you're at a point in your career where learning from a boss is something you really want, and this potential boss sounds like someone with something to teach. You happen to have lost an uncle to cancer recently and are moved by this CEO's dedication to raising money for cancer research. You also happen to be a runner who has run several half-marathons and would be open to joining in for the chief's annual charity run. You hope to make your future in Boston; and if you do a good job for this CEO, you might have a well-connected ally in the city for years to come.

By carefully reviewing just those details on LinkedIn and developing a source who knows your potential boss, you now know a great deal about that individual, what makes them tick, how they run their team. You also have an inkling of the upsides and downsides to working for them. You have gotten there just by reviewing what is on LinkedIn—you haven't even run a wider search on the internet or seen what could be gleaned from other social media.

The point of all this work is to prepare deeply for your interview and to develop a strategy to connect with this person—and to be able to aptly convey what your concerns are. Perhaps you're concerned about work/life balance with such a hard-charging, serious boss, and you use some of your elicitation skills to see if you can subtly draw out from them the expectations for daily hours and whether working nights or weekends is ever a reality. Asking such questions directly might make such a person wonder about your commitment to the job, so collecting that intelligence in a more circumspect manner—by using the elicitation skills we have gone over—would be more to your advantage.

Let's say you're a bit more advanced in your career and you're starting to develop opportunities to sit on boards, which can be lucrative and prestigious. Your professional experience and your personality have made you a good candidate for these roles, and you want to pick and choose carefully which boards you might sit on. Time, after all, is a valuable resource to you, and your professional experience and leadership traits give you the discretion to be choosy.

Let's say you've done all the LinkedIn work I have described, and you're trying to develop a profile of the person—our "CEO"—you're going to interview for a board position with. Let's go even further and discuss incorporating the lessons we have already learned in earlier chapters as we add some new twists to evaluating your counterpart—who is the CEO of the company whose board you might join—and whether the opportunity is right for you.

Recall the lessons from Chapter 3 about Atmosphere and Intangibles. Now we're going to use them to glean insights into the CEO and what the offices of the company you might join look like.

On his LinkedIn page, and in a lot of his public photos, the CEO is conservatively dressed. But when he walks into the conference room to meet with you, he's wearing a black T-shirt and jeans, fashionable sneakers, silver hair slicked back but not parted as carefully as in those public photos. It's consistent with what you noticed walking into the offices—people mostly in business casual.

The CEO greets you warmly and comments on the cappuccino his assistant has prepared for you from the coffee bar. He tells you the company has revamped elements of their office culture to reflect a changing workforce—business casual attire is now accepted, the company added that popular coffee bar near reception, and the business has embraced flexible work, with occasional remote work being more acceptable.

You take all this in and realize you're entering an environment in flux. The CEO—an accomplished individual who has worked for top companies for decades—seems genuinely committed to change. He talks about the desire for a board that will help propel these changes to corporate culture—which the CEO views as not only about attracting top talent but also about increasing performance.

All this is exciting to you and dovetails with your professional interests and goals for being on a board, but you notice you've been with the CEO for a while now and, aside from some cursory questions to open things up, he's been on his soapbox talking about these things and not asking you any questions.

You notice that the CEO walked into the room with a folder of papers and spread them out before you on the table. At the beginning of the conversation, he moved aside a bottle of water that had been placed on the table by his assistant in order to spread those papers out widely before leaning forward on the table and expounding on the company, the cultural changes it has undertaken, and what he's looking for in terms of board development.

Finally it's your turn to talk, and you notice some changes in the CEO's behavior. When you speak, he moves from a posture of leaning forward to one that is spread out, legs splayed open, arms on the nearby chairs, taking up a lot of space. Often, while you're speaking, the CEO breaks eye contact and consults those spread-out papers.

What does such behavior mean? When evaluating behavior, no one particular movement or posture always means one thing. Some behaviors and postures have a higher correlation to certain things, but it's essential to establish context to put them in perspective and gain insight. What's critical to evaluating behavior is to establish a baseline behavior and then observe the changes in your target and what might have triggered them.

In this case, the CEO has established a baseline behavior for his own speech with a forward-leaning posture (which you mirrored). But once you leaned further forward and started speaking, the CEO leaned back, which might indicate a lack of respect—not mirroring your forward-leaning posture. But what is more telling is the fact that the CEO spread his legs widely and then spread his arms out on the chairs nearby. That is known as territorial behavior, and while it might sound like something you hear on a nature documentary, it's something that humans engage in.

The CEO began that behavior at this interview by spreading his papers out on the table, showing that this space is spoken for—it's the first display of dominance. The CEO's initial soliloquy on the company and its changes, where you noted that he went on for quite some time without offering you a chance to speak, furthers this impression. The posture of the CEO's legs and arms, taking up more physical space, is sending a message to you. That message is: *Sure, I'm interested in learning whether you're a good fit for my board. You seem to have qualifications that are interesting to me; that's the only reason I'm in this room. But I want you to know that if you're affiliated with this company, I call the shots. I might want your expertise, but I want it on my terms.*

How should you react to this sort of behavior if you're trying to build rapport? Adam,* the military interrogator, would adjust his mirroring based in part on his target's status. "If he has lieutenant bars on his uniform and I'm mirroring him, I will likely hurt myself in building rapport because that person already views me as having a lower status than him. In that case, I'm going to be a bit more distant, calm, and make myself somewhat smaller to make him comfortable. If he is in a lower role, say a cook, I can loom, I can be a bit bigger."

Again, context is key, and nothing about the mission of rapport-building and reading people should be formulaic. It's a good idea to mirror someone . . . until it's not. Mirroring the behavior of the CEO displaying territorial behavior would be counterproductive.

In this interview, you're taking in information and evaluating the CEO just as much as the CEO is evaluating you. Is he going to be a good person to work with, and is this board seat the right opportunity for you?

You note that as you're sitting directly across from the CEO, speaking about your leadership experience and the vastly different corporate environments you have worked in, he picks up the bottle of water and, after taking a sip, puts it back down in front of him. Instead of returning to the arms/legs splayed combination, he crosses his arms.

The CEO has just engaged in what's known as blocking behavior. Anytime someone puts anything between you and them, think *blocking behavior*. In this case, the folded arms create even a degree of blocking you as you're speaking. The bottle placed down in front of you, seemingly a minor thing, is telling as well.

Think about an opposite scenario. You're going out to dinner with a close friend you haven't seen in a while. You arrive, and after greetings you sit down at the restaurant table. You notice that your friend takes the napkin, which had been placed in front of her in a folded tent, and places it on her lap. But she also moves aside a candle that's in the middle of the table, as well as the water and wineglasses between you; even the salt and pepper shakers get pushed aside. She is clearing the area in front of you and doing the opposite of blocking—she wants a clear lane between you, nothing obstructing you at all.

Blocking behaviors can manifest themselves in a variety of ways. When people hear news they don't like, they close their eyes and often pinch the area at the bridge of their nose. These actions can be subtle; but if you note the context and the change from baseline behavior, you will recognize patterns and start to deduce *reasons* for behavioral changes and the *messages* behind them.

Back at the board-seat interview, you've shared your views on things; and at this point, you notice something about the CEO's fancy sneakers. The CEO has now sat back, crossed his legs, and angled those kicks toward the door. You wouldn't be wrong in thinking that the CEO has decided he's done with this meeting and is looking to exit the conversation. In any conversation, notice how someone has angled their body; if you're talking to someone who isn't facing you directly, it's not a bad assumption that the person is looking to exit the conversation. Often it can be just the feet that are pointed away from you—that's enough of a clue to reveal how the person is feeling about you and the conversation you're having.

So, what have you gleaned from the conversation with the CEO and the visit to the office? You've noted that the company atmosphere is one you've come to enjoy—a more casual environment where employees can get good coffee and have flexibility in their life to achieve at work but also thrive personally. But while the CEO seems passionate about these changes, and that is a positive to you, you saw some major red flags about the CEO as an individual. You've determined that this CEO might be something of an egomaniac who only wants to listen to his own counsel, but also someone who seems to surround himself with a board and staff that will reinforce his views and goals. This CEO doesn't seem like someone who wants to really understand different perspectives and occasionally be challenged. The CEO's body language while you were speaking was borderline disrespectful, and you wonder whether behind his ebullient personality and casual dress lurks a petty person who can disregard people as quickly as he acquires them.

Let's go back to our FBI counterintelligence interview (see pages 126 through 127) and push further into what body language can reveal to us.

The FBI agent in this interview—and this applies to law-enforcement situations across the board—closely watches the interview subject because *the body reveals what the mind conceals.* Our bodies give us away in interactions, and while we've noted that no one gesture means one thing only, the person who consistently pays attention to body language and context, trying to establish a baseline behavior for comparison's sake, will understand their counterpart and what they might be thinking but not revealing.

In this interview, the FBI agent will carefully watch (and potentially review later on video) how the subject physically responds to questions. The agent is even looking for micro-gestures and soothing gestures. Micro-gestures are fleeting, involuntary behaviors in response to external stimulus, and soothing gestures are small actions that every human does to calm themselves. It could be subtle, like the stroking of your legs or licking your lips. Sometimes it's more overt, like rubbing your neck. But, again, if you note a subject's baseline, you'll start to see patterns. What was the person doing right before you asked the question, and how did they respond when you asked it? Did they smile broadly and lean in with their answer? Or did they start rubbing their neck after a quick licking of their lips?

## DETECTING DECEPTION

Now that we've started reading body language, we're ready to enter the somewhat controversial subject of detecting deception. In my corporate-world work, I've seen former CIA case officers, FBI agents, and other government officials set themselves up in private practice and then pitch themselves to companies as able to train their teams to be "human lie detectors." Most experts in the area call bullshit, lie-detection being an exaggeration of the effectiveness of techniques to sniff out deceptive behavior. They believe that no person can definitively tell when another person is lying with a high degree of consistency, especially someone they don't know well. People are just too different, and not even a polygraph machine is right all the time.

It doesn't mean that trying to detect deceptive behavior is a lost cause. On the contrary, there is a lot that anyone can do to note certain behaviors that *might* indicate deception. Sometimes these behaviors might not indicate deception, but might instead indicate stress or anxiety, which is also an interesting data point.

In our business and everyday interactions, we want to believe that the person we're dealing with is being straight with us. Nobody wants to go through life being suspicious of everyone around them.

But understanding the subtle ways that people might seek to shade the truth or hide feelings of discomfort—if not outright deceive—around certain subjects can be a helpful way to navigate interpersonal relations. What's that old Cold War saying? *Trust, but verify.* I say give people the benefit of the doubt, but I keep an eye out for deceptive behavior.

So, let's talk about some of the clues you can pick up in a conversation that might indicate dishonesty.

*Failure to Answer or Understand a Question*

The example that I give at conferences and to teams when I give trainings is from the sports world. I remind the sports fans in the audience about future Hall of Fame quarterback Tom Brady and the Deflategate scandal. In this imbroglio, the New England Patriots were accused of slightly deflating the football to make the pigskin easier to handle and give an advantage to their vaunted gunslinger. As the issue was unfolding, a journalist asked Tom if he had anything to do with deflating the footballs. Tom answered, "I would never do anything outside of the rules of play."

Now, that answer doesn't mean that Tom Brady is actually a cheater, full stop. But it indicates what is typically deceptive behavior, because he didn't really answer the question. He could have said "I had nothing to do with deflating any footballs. I knew nothing about it." But his answer is slippery and indicates that he might be trying to rationalize the situation and preserve his squeaky-clean image.

Another cautionary flag is someone's failure to *understand* the question. When I witness someone respond this way, it is usually embarrassing and painful. The person does a double-take when asked something that they clearly don't want to deal with, and their brain acts like it can't compute. "What do you mean," or some variation thereof, is often the reply, as if they couldn't possibly understand the question, which they might perceive as an accusation, and they just bat it back to you without an answer.

Both actions here are indications that the person is not being truthful.

### Qualifiers and Non-Answer Statements

Let's say you're the CSO of an organization and there has been a theft from the petty cash kept in the office. Hundreds of dollars are missing. There are only a few suspects—those who have access to the cash and were in the office at the time it's been determined that the cash went missing. One person, we'll call him Larry, seems to be the primary suspect, and you're questioning him.

You ask Larry directly: "Did you take the money from the petty cash drawer?" and he replies "You know, I thought you might ask that question. Listen, at our company petty cash is used for a wide variety of things. We buy cakes when someone has a birthday, we sometimes use that money to buy toner for the printer. . . ." and he goes on, rambling without directly answering the question.

Larry has started off with a qualifier—"I thought you might ask that question"—and that is where the alarm bells should start going off. If Larry is innocent, he wouldn't be getting coy with you regarding such a serious matter and accusation. He would simply say "No, I didn't take the money."

But Larry qualifies, and then goes on from there with a rambling soliloquy about the usage of petty cash. Perhaps Larry is rationalizing his taking the money, maybe trying to say that because the money is used for such a wide variety of purposes, his taking it as a temporary loan wasn't a big deal. Regardless, when you're faced with someone qualifying their answer at the beginning of a statement—which could be used to buy time as the liar builds up a head of steam—and then rambling on without answering the direct question you have put to them, you've gotten a pretty good indication that the person is not being truthful.

*Repeating the Question*

We've all seen this one. You ask someone a question, and they do a double-take and say "Excuse me?" and you repeat the question for them. Or you ask them a question and they look around the room and repeat the question out loud, as if the answers to the question are floating in the air of the room.

Don't condemn the person as a liar yet! I'm half deaf, and sometimes I miss a question and need it repeated. I promise I'm not engaged in any sort of chicanery when I do so. Perhaps the question came as a surprise to an innocent person and they need to hear it again to process it because it's shocking to them. Perhaps it's a complicated question and the person on the receiving end was deep in thought about the subject of the previous questions or whatever other conversation was going on.

Still, question-repeats are a strategy used by liars, often to buy time. By asking to have the question repeated or repeating it themselves and musing about it, they are buying their mind a few precious moments to calculate an answer. So, while the tactic in itself—just like so much of deception detection—isn't a foolproof indication of guilt, it is a warning sign to notice and contextualize with the other details you're ascertaining from the person.

*Invoking Oaths*

Ah, the classic mafia tactic. Picture a gangster looking to swear to the veracity of what he's saying, to throw off his fellow gangsters who think he might have betrayed them. "I swear on the eyes of my children," he tells his fellow bad guys.

In the mafioso's case, the language and its intensity might be warranted—his compatriots are a violent gang that don't take kindly to betrayal. He needs to be vehement in his denial. But in the real world, such vehemence is often an indication of dishonesty. If you're questioning Larry and he didn't take the petty cash, you're likely to hear "No, I had nothing to do with the missing money." If he says "I swear on my mother's grave!" you might have a problem with Larry. Such exaggerated language is often an effort to throw off the accuser—*wow, Larry certainly is passionate in his denial*—but the smarter interrogator knows the oath as a natural tactic of a guilty mind.

Remember, such a strong denial is not in itself an overwhelming indication of guilt. In these situations, people find themselves all worked up, upset over being caught up in something unpleasant, and adamant about declaring their innocence. But a guilty person, one who is more shameless and not dodging questions, will often use some of these behaviors to hide from the truth.

## DETECTING NONVERBAL DECEPTION

Remember that the body reveals what the mind conceals. Let's talk about some ways to detect deception by looking at how aspects of our body language are often more truthful than the words that we speak.

*Verbal/Nonverbal Disconnect*

As we saw earlier, sometimes the body will directly contradict what a person is saying. Law-enforcement officials often have some version of a story involving someone they've called in for an interview on a case. That person might not even be a suspect, and they might have gotten through their interview without triggering any suspicion. But when the interview is over and they are being escorted out, sometimes their body language gives them away. "Thanks for coming down to the precinct today. If we have some more questions, would you mind coming back in, later this week?" The person then says "Oh, sure, that's no problem." But while making the "no problem" statement, they are shaking their head. So while their verbal language is *Yes,* their body language is shouting out *No!*

*Voice Cracking, Coldness, and Fidgeting*

Let's go back to our FBI counterintelligence interview. Our agent is asking the subject carefully planned questions, looking for contradictions in the statements they have already given, details that might contradict the story of another suspect, or clues in their verbal and nonverbal body language that might indicate deception or a high degree of stress, which often look similar.

Our agent notes several times when she asks the subject a question and they start to fidget with the plastic water bottle our agent has been savvy enough to place on the table. Law enforcement will often put an item near an interview subject—a water bottle, a paper clip, a rubber band—to see what questions make that subject fidget with the object, which is a soothing motion, and note which question triggered that behavior. They also often put a subject on a chair with wheels to watch which question leads the subject to start moving around for similar reasons.

When the subject answers questions, our agent notices that in several instances his voice cracks. When the body is under stress, our mouths dry up. That's why you see people moving their tongue around their mouths, swallowing a lot, and licking their lips. And it's the reason the voice cracks—because the vocal pathway has gotten so dry, due to stress.

During the interview, the agent notices that the subject is hugging himself at times and seems to shiver. She, meanwhile, is perfectly comfortable with the temperature in the room. In fact, she was in this room with colleagues shortly before the interview began, and nobody complained about the temperature or indicated that they were cold. She knows that feeling cold in a room that everyone else deems comfortable is another clue that the subject is under a high degree of stress. Another symptom of the body being under great stress is a sense of coldness. The body is working extra-hard under this stress, and precious blood is not reaching our outer layers as efficiently as it normally would.

Our agent can put together the symptoms: fidgeting after specific questions, voice cracking, manifestations of coldness. While anyone might feel uncomfortable being interviewed by the FBI, this person, she deduces, is likely either lying or not fully revealing what they know. They are manifesting deceptive behavior. The agent will then take further steps to consider where this person fits into her goal of getting to the bottom of her case.

The stakes aren't nearly as high in our work lives or everyday lives when we're speaking with someone. But I bet that in reading these previous paragraphs about deceptive behavior, you have tied them to situations and specific individuals you've encountered. These behaviors don't specifically condemn our targets to a particular verdict, but they should inform our business and social interactions. They help us better understand who we are talking to and whether they are being candid with us.

## DEALING WITH DECEPTION

Before Steve Romano became a hostage negotiator for the FBI, he worked in counterintelligence. An assignment he had at the end of the Cold War provides a good example of properly dealing with deceptive behavior. His first goal when dealing with any case he was assigned was to gain a deeper understanding of what had happened; second was to handle the punishment of the behavior.

With the Soviet Union falling apart, it was as though a light had been turned on and all the cockroaches were scrambling for cover. The FBI had its hands full of newly unearthed plots and scandals, now that the Soviets were no longer pulling the strings. The U.S. embassy in Bulgaria proved to have a great example of such a case.

It had come out that many of the local staff were working with Bulgaria's secret police. Foreign nationals—usually citizens of the country in which the embassy or consulate is located—make up a huge portion of the staff of any U.S. embassy or consulate, and the U.S. government depends on these individuals to keep the business of diplomacy running. But Bulgarian spies had effectively co-opted a solid portion of the U.S. embassy's local staff, and now the FBI had to get to the bottom of what had happened, how much and what kind of secrets were leaked. The FBI was able to ascertain a particular subset of the local staff to place under suspicion, and Steve was called in from Washington to lead the interrogation of these individuals.

Steve's goal was, again, to find out who had revealed what and what secrets had been leaked. It wasn't his job to mete out punishments for these individuals. He was empowered to speak of clemency in return for cooperation because, while the U.S. government might seek some form of accountability from its former employees, the main thing was protecting aspects of national security that might have been made vulnerable because of these leaks.

To focus on this specific goal, Steve used an FBI tactic known as Rationalize, Project, and Minimize (RPM). He sat down with the subjects and said the following:

"We know that you were cooperating with the local security service and leaking information from this embassy. While we're very disappointed in that, we are more focused on finding out what happened than on retribution. We understand you were placed under a great deal of pressure. We know that the local service pressured you by making threats against you and your family. We know that they also offered powerful inducements to cooperate—we're aware of your family moving to a nicer apartment a few years ago and your children being placed in special schools. We understand that the pressure must have been intense and that you had to do what was best for your family. I'm certain that whatever you shared were only small details and no one got hurt. But we really need to know exactly what happened and specifically what you shared over the years, even if you think these details were minor. If you work with us, I promise things will turn out much better for you and your family."

So Steve rationalized the betrayal of the employee: "We know that the local service pressured you by making threats against you and your family." He projected: "We know that they also offered powerful inducements to cooperate—we're aware of your family moving to a nicer apartment a few years ago and your children being placed in special schools." And he minimized the impact of the betrayal: "I'm certain that whatever you shared were only small details and no one got hurt."

With that approach, Steve and his team secured the cooperation of just about every one of the suspects, and the U.S. government was able to take steps to minimize the damage done to national security.

The RPM approach is highly useful in corporate settings as well.

Let's turn our attention back to Larry, the petty-cash thief. He has given his qualifier to our CSO and then rambled on with his non-answer statement. Now the CSO drops the bomb on him. There is security footage of him entering the office where the petty cash is kept. The act was captured on film Friday evening, right before the weekend started. It's time to use the RPM method to resolve this situation, get rid of Larry, and move the company forward with new security protocols.

"Listen, Larry, please don't pull my leg any more about this— we know you took the money. But look, I get it. I've been told that you're going through a divorce, and I heard you had a big weekend blowing off steam with this money. I'm not saying it's okay, but I get it. I've been through hard times, too, and I know sometimes you need to blow off steam, and I get that the divorce has impacted your financial situation. But, Larry, borrowing company funds for personal reasons, even if you planned to pay it back, is just not okay. There are ways that this can escalate that we all want to avoid and just move on; but it's critical that you confess to this before we can work together to put this behind us."

The CSO's laying his cards on the table in this way leads to Larry's tearful confession, and it was directly because the CSO used empathy to project Larry's action and get inside Larry's head and help him rationalize what he had done. He then minimized the repercussions without completely throwing them away. This point is critical. If the CSO started making threats about calling the police, Larry could have dug his heels in and said he was getting a lawyer, which would have made the situation much trickier, extended this corporate standoff, and cost the company even more money.

The CSO also used *soft language* when describing things. He didn't use the word "steal": instead he used "borrowing," projecting into Larry's head a potential rationalization for his behavior. If you're the chief financial officer of a company that's just uncovered fraud in your business and you're speaking to the suspect, you're going to have a better chance of getting a confession to "financial irregularities" than you are to the big, bad word "fraud," which is loaded with criminal repercussions and social opprobrium. Using soft language is an excellent strategy when seeking the truth from someone.

The CSO also continued to use Larry's name strategically throughout the encounter. It shows Larry some respect and empathy, that he gets that Larry's life is messy at the moment. Remember what FBI hostage negotiators always talk about—the person ended the siege because they felt understood and listened to. The CSO is going to end this messy situation—without lawyers and the police getting involved—by demonstrating empathy, by using the RPM method, by keeping his voice calm and measured, and not by hurling accusations and threats. People threatened and accused tend to double down on their behavior, not acquiesce.

## KEY TAKEAWAYS

FBI agents and other government officials are highly trained in the use of "skills of social influence" to subtly shift the dynamics of everything from a tense hostage standoff to an interview with a subject. Keep these key points in mind to navigate a variety of social and business interactions to create the best opportunity for you to succeed.

1.  Defuse difficult encounters by using a quieter and slower tone of voice, by allowing the other person to vent, by avoiding taking offense, and by identifying whether the cause of the

challenging encounter is about the situation or about you specifically.

2.  Despite what some business books and gurus tell you, negotiation shouldn't be a zero-sum game. Humiliating your counterpart or leaving them with a bad deal is not the way to cultivate durable relationships. Assess the other side's motivation, get them into the habit of cooperating, and use empathy to create a win-win dynamic.

3.  When interviewing, information is your best friend, and you should prepare by gathering even the smallest of details to put you in a position to succeed. Think carefully about the context of the interview to judge what it is you want to help chart a path to get there.

4.  No one is a human lie detector, but you can identify red flags when someone might be engaged in deceptive behavior. Use the RPM method (Rationalize, Project, and Minimize) to create the best outcome when dealing with someone you've identified as engaged in bad behavior.

# 5

## DISGUISES, SUPERPOWERS, AND OTHER SPY-DEVELOPMENT METHODS

*Techniques from Spies for Salespeople to Get to Yes*

When Bob Grenier was based in a North African country in the 1980s, he was tasked with penetrating leftist student organizations. It was the height of the Cold War, and his superiors wanted to understand how these organizations worked, who their leaders were, and what their relationship was like with the Soviets.

But Bob had little to go on, because no one had penetrated these organizations yet. The internet hadn't been invented. The organizations weren't exactly advertising an org chart.

So Bob needed to get creative.

He got a beat-up car, dressed like he was a student himself (which he could pull off still being a young man), and he drove to where the students hung out. He learned that the students tended to hitchhike to get around, and so he made it a habit to pick them up. He would chat them up in his fluent French, and if he determined that a particular student didn't have anything for him, he'd pass him a pack of local cigarettes and let the student find another ride. But if his attempts to elicit information yielded something interesting, he knew he was on the right course.

That is how Bob was able to penetrate the paranoid, budding Communist youth in that Muslim country. He did it by adjusting his looks, his personality, and his approach.

We in the sales world can take similar steps to overcome hurdles and find success. I'm going to tell you about how I did exactly that at one point in my career. No, I'm not going to have you wear a disguise, though you might wind up adjusting your appearance based on some of the case studies and ideas I'm about to share.

But before we dive further into these outside-the-box methods, let's talk about spies in disguise.

Unlike a lot of the falsehoods Hollywood spouts about spies, the part about operatives utilizing disguises is the rare detail that Hollywood gets right. If we use a wider aperture on the idea, we can learn from the way that spies utilize their cover; and if we zoom in from there, we can see how they shape their personalities and approaches based on disguise.

The use of disguise in intelligence-gathering is as old as espionage itself, which is known as "the world's second-oldest profession." Disguise essentially serves two different purposes: either to make you look like another specific person, or just not like yourself. Because photography has only been a part of our world for a comparatively short time, disguise has historically focused on turning the spy into another type of person. A spy in ancient times sent to penetrate another group would adopt the dress of that other tribe to blend in. Because there were no photographs to compare someone to, or databases to track their personal details, if the spy could blend in, they could largely carry it off.

What betrayed those spies, and still does betray them, is having incriminating evidence on their person. That's what did in Major John André—the spy who recruited Benedict Arnold. He was caught by American soldiers, and what caused his downfall was not a poor disguise, but that he was found with incriminating documents in the bottoms of his shoes. For similar reasons, British paratroopers who were dropping behind Nazi lines in World War II and were to adopt local dress once on the ground declined their government's offer of the latest gadgets that their service had developed. They knew that having any sort of equipment like that would be prima facie evidence of espionage.

Spy historian H. Keith Welton claims that the first instance of a spy being caught in disguise by advancement in technology was during the Civil War. A Northern commander had pictures of his team taken, and in one of the photos he found a person he didn't know, and he knew *everyone* in his unit. His unit had been penetrated by a Southern spy.

But outward appearance is only the first aspect of disguise. As Welton points out, "Sometimes it is much easier to do a physical disguise than it is to change a person's mindset. When Tony Mendez—the hero of the film *Argo*—was taking the American diplomats to the airport in Tehran to be covertly evacuated, his challenge was to make them appear to be a Canadian film crew rather than buttoned-down American diplomats to the suspicious Iranian authorities. The physical side with the disguise was easier than changing the diplomats' mindset—their walk and gait, their accents, etc."

This story hints at another aspect of disguise: how closely the CIA has collaborated with Hollywood over the years.

Hollywood, with its enormous film budgets, is at the vanguard of what is possible to shape the appearance of a person.

And the entertainment industry regularly collaborates with the CIA to share cutting-edge aspects of the disguise tradecraft it has developed.

The British spy agency MI5 has at times also leaned on the vaunted theater industry in its country to help its disguise capabilities. As Welton points out, "Good tradecraft will always reflect the best tech available at the time." Spy agencies will get creative and collaborative in order to access that technology.

The CIA takes the idea of disguise so seriously that there is a position within the Agency called chief of disguises. Typically, the way the Agency approaches disguises is to classify them as either light disguise or heavy disguise. Light disguises subtly change your appearance—think wigs, glasses, fake facial hair. Heavy disguises drastically alter your appearance and/or physicality.

For a heavy disguise, the Agency might wrap something around your knee or put something in your shoe to give you a limp. They might take an impression of your teeth and gums and craft something you can place in your mouth that will alter your cheeks and how your face looks. They can make a woman appear pregnant. They can add a gnarly mole to your face that will capture the attention of people and perhaps distract them from some other aspect of what a spy really looks like.

But despite access to Hollywood's sorcery, there are of course limits to disguise tradecraft. It can make a shorter person taller, but not a taller person shorter. And while the Agency feels it can turn a woman into a man, it doesn't feel it can credibly turn a man into a woman.

Let's talk about some scenarios in which a spy might want to adopt a disguise.

If you're a spy in Pakistan and you are meeting an agent in the country's dangerous North-West Frontier territories, your disguise needs are different than a spy attempting to cross a hostile border with a fake passport. Your primary concern is your safety, and your goal is to not draw attention to yourself.

You're going to want to case out the café where you'll be meeting your source. Once there, you'll want to assess means of egress in case there is a dangerous situation that requires a quick escape, and you'll observe the other patrons to get a sense of what the typical customer base is like. You can make a determination about whether the café patrons are simple everyday people, or a rougher, sketchier crowd, and plan accordingly. So you put on a traditional *shalwar kameez,* and put on a beard and change your hair as you sip tea in the café getting a sense of things.

Or perhaps you're a non-official cover officer based in Frankfurt posing as a Danish businessperson. You have to meet an agent with important intelligence to share in transit in Germany, and the meeting place is a restaurant not far from your home. You've been to this restaurant with friends, and you don't want to bump into any of them, because you'll be doing the meeting under a different name. So you put on a wig and glasses, which is just enough to plant doubts in the mind of a friend who might see you. But that's not enough—you're going to have to remember that while Americans tend to cut their food with the knife in their dominant hand and the fork in the other, and then shift the fork to their dominant hand to eat, Europeans tend to cut and eat without shifting the utensils. All part of the disguises, and the details can be critical.

Do you remember the scene from the Quentin Tarantino movie *Inglourious Basterds* when the British agent is dressed as a Nazi in a basement bar as part of a rendezvous with their agent, a beautiful and well-known German actress? He and his compatriots have the misfortune of choosing a bar where a few Nazis are carousing, and they are accosted by a Nazi officer who is suspicious of the group. Tarantino builds the suspense as the Nazi questions the group and the British agent in particular, who claims he is from a particular region in Austria. Seemingly satisfied, the British officer blows his cover when he signals the number three with his fingers. But he's done it the wrong way. The Nazi knows that anyone from that region holds up different fingers when signaling three. A horrible gunfight in Tarantino fashion erupts, and everyone but the German actress is killed. Obviously, that's a Hollywood dramatization, but it's a good example of how important it is to get the little details of your cover right.

You might be reading this and thinking, *This is all interesting stuff, Jeremy, but what does it have to do with my sales career?*

Let's look at a couple of sales scenarios.

## SCENARIO 1: THE BAD DAY

We all have bad days. But what do you do when you have to be *on* during one of those bad days?

Let's say it's approaching 5 p.m. and you're scheduled to meet clients for happy-hour drinks. This is the junior team from an important account. The annual renewal of their retainer agreement is coming up in a few months, and you have to keep them engaged, keep them using your research services. You happen to know that a competitor—a scrappy upstart who is undercutting you on pricing in the market and whose team is hustling hard and doing good work—has now infiltrated this client and is focused on pushing you out, or least capturing the greater share of the client's work. While the senior decision-maker remains a target of influence, it is the junior team members who are in the trenches every day making use of your service, making daily choices about whether they will call your team or the competitor on a new project. You can talk about your firm's greater experience in serving the market all you want, and you can develop a close relationship with the head of the team. But let's face it, you know that your service isn't really that different from this upstart competitor, and if her team is telling her that the scrappy competitor is doing work as good as your more expensive firm, it might not matter that she likes you. She has to make good decisions about her business. It's all a threat to your renewal changes and therefore your quota.

You can't let your bad day influence this happy hour. You have to be on your game, making those junior team members like you, feel a kinship for you, because the next day, when they are about to pick up the phone to call a research analyst, the reason why they call your analyst versus the competitor's might only be that they like you more.

But you've had four grueling pitches today, three of which didn't go well at all. You had a big fight that morning with your spouse after sleeping badly. Maybe there are other storm clouds on the horizon of your personal life. The point is—you're not in your best mental mindset to go meet your clients and be at your most collegial. You really want to just go home and flop down on the couch and watch mindless TV.

How do you step up your game and meet that challenge?

## SCENARIO 2: THE ARROGANT CLIENT

You're going to meet a new prospect. It's a multi-billion-dollar hedge fund. It could be any big, powerful target client, but let's work with the hedge-fund scenario. These guys are enormously successful and powerful.

You've been chasing them for a while, trying to get a meeting, knowing that if you impress them and they start using your services it could change your whole sales year. It would also be a prestigious feather in your cap.

But the contact you've been chasing is arrogant and has been reluctant to meet. He's finally agreed to give you a half hour of his time, and you arrive to a powerhouse office (see Chapter 3 and the discussion about Atmosphere and Intangibles). The beautiful but cold receptionist seems to be sitting beneath a Rothko; the rest of the high-end, minimalist furniture seems like artwork as well.

You have one shot to impress this dismissive prospect. You know that they have worked with a competitor for many years, so this will not be easy. You need to get past their prickly persona and use some real skill to supplant such an entrenched competitor.

How do you rise to the occasion to meet these challenges?

## THE *MAD MEN* METHOD

*Mad Men* is one of my all-time favorite TV shows. The writing, acting, set direction . . . it's high art. I've watched the entire seven seasons several times, and I think there are golden nuggets in the show about a life in business, and specifically sales. Two characters in particular have been extremely useful to me at different times.

Roger Sterling and Don Draper are flip sides of a coin, completely different personalities and approaches, but equally effective. What I'm suggesting here is that either of these characters can be useful in the situations—the bad day and the arrogant client—that I've described, that putting on a disguise and masquerading as them can help you prevail on these challenging assignments.

Learning to embody characters you admire can be a powerful way to rise to a challenge. It's a disguise method that seeks to subtly refine aspects of our personalities to meet the moment.

Perhaps you're reading this and thinking *Jeremy, didn't you say it's about connection and not deception? Aren't you suggesting we deceive someone with this method?*

Not at all! Do you remember the Walt Whitman quote? *"Do I contradict myself? Very well then, I contradict myself. I am large, I contain multitudes."*

This method of disguise leverages your multitudes to bring out your best self. Many actors talk about how some of their best roles were for parts that they could really see themselves in. Spies know this: according to Marc Polymeropoulos, espionage is "an acting job."

What I'm suggesting here is *tweaking* your personality dials— amplifying certain sides of your personality at one time and then de-emphasizing others at another.

Let's start with Scenario 1—the bad day along with the unwanted happy hour. We're going to put on our Roger Sterling mask to overcome our horrible day and meet the moment.

What's Roger Sterling like? He's outgoing, fun, gregarious, quick-witted; he is that silver fox at the cocktail reception that people congregate around. Roger Sterling loves to entertain clients, and they love to go out with him, but he always has his eye on the prize: winning a new client or keeping the existing one happy.

As 5 p.m. approaches and you're headed to that client happy hour, you're steeling yourself for the next hour or two by putting on your Roger Sterling mask. It allows you to put aside your exhaustion, your frustration at the day, your desire to go sit in a quiet, dark room and think about anything but work. It allows you to preserve your humanity and not feel like a fraud, and it pushes aside the desire to complain about your day to these clients, or reveal just how exhausted and frustrated you are.

Instead, with your Roger Sterling mask on you can be *that guy*. You can buy the rounds, and clink the glasses, crack the jokes, gently chiding the group that they better call your research analysts tomorrow morning. You will have spent the time before the happy hour going over the extensive notes you've taken working with these clients, reminding yourself of the particularities of their firm, their work habits, and then, at an even more granular level, of the individuals that you think will be there, where they went to college, what sports teams they follow, everything unique about them that you have tracked so far.

All these things arm you with the ammunition you need to make this happy hour a success. It allows you to be the best of yourself by putting on a mask that isn't a phony rendering of a you that's not you, but rather one that allows you to draw forth the side of your personality that is definitely there but had just been buried that day by life's travails.

Let's talk about Scenario 2—the arrogant client—and how I would conjure my inner Don Draper for this mission.

Let's describe Don Draper first. He's charismatic, he has gravitas; he isn't outgoing and loquacious; but, because of the qualities I mentioned, people tend to hang on every word he says, and every word he says seems to matter, as if he has some inner thought editor who culls his sentences until they feel like they've been carved in stone. He inspires respect by those around him and he doesn't suffer fools.

So that morning you put on your best suit, your favorite skinny tie, and you stiffen your spine as the elevator dings and you walk into the posh lobby, your leather shoes clinking on the porcelain floor. The frosty receptionist doesn't bother you at all. In fact, you don't even notice—such things don't even hit your radar screen. The décor of the office leaves you unfazed—you simply belong.

When you meet your arrogant target, you're not full of gratitude for his taking the meeting, nor are you back-slapping, joking around, asking him about his golf game or weekend plans. You're a serious person on an important mission. You won't be distracted or deterred. Your whole attitude is that you have something really valuable—that you yourself are the key to this value—and if this target isn't smart enough to see it, or if he is too arrogant to accept it, that's his loss. You won't be singing and dancing for your supper. They are lucky that you're here.

You are *selling as a peer* that day. You walk into that room with that investor—who focuses on companies doing business in emerging markets—knowing that you have a deep background in these markets as well. You have helped investors make money in these areas. You know that you can help this person too. If this prospect across from you doesn't want to see that, it's his loss.

(If you're walking into a meeting and not ready to sell as a peer, you need to do some more homework and understand your client and market better.)

Beginning a meeting by inviting the client to talk about their work is always a good place to start. You can adjust your pitch accordingly and not spend time describing something your company provides if they start off by noting that that particular area is not of interest. But in this case you start the meeting off asking if you can share a case study. This is one of my favorite Don Draper methods: *leveraging storytelling in the pitch*. You're there to talk to them about leveraging your firm's intelligence-gathering capabilities so they can make better-informed trades. You tell them about an extraordinary recent case—perhaps it was putting a local agent of yours on the top of a hill in some far-flung part of the world in front of a mine's entrance for a few days to count the number of trucks entering and exiting the mine, how heavily laden they were, and other details. The goal was to get a sense of average daily output and what kind of production this publicly traded company is getting from this mine. Whatever the story is, it's carefully chosen and has just enough detail about tradecraft and what competitors can do wrong (and get the client in trouble) that it plants the seed of how much better your firm is than the competitor.

You use the fear of missing out (FOMO) as well with your case study. Your work counting the number of trucks coming out of the mine gave your client a much better estimate of the mining company's quarterly earnings than the average retail investor. The only thing close to a joke you make at the meeting is that while your fees weren't cheap for such an assignment in a far-flung part of the world, they were merely the equivalent to a rounding error in the profit that this rival hedge fund made. That does a few things for you: it signals the premium nature of your work and that it's not cheap (and this prepares the conversation to turn to fees, if you get there). And it places FOMO at the center of things. The arrogant client doesn't want to lose out on making a bundle working with your firm when a competitor is doing so.

Throughout the meeting, you dial back your natural gregariousness—this client doesn't want to be your friend. You try to make every word matter, make sure you're careful in your replies, sober in your thinking. Most of all, you continue to exude that you *matter*, that you have ways to help them make more money.

## SPOTTING

Have you ever arrived at a business mixer, perhaps some kind of cocktail reception, and walked into the room with dozens, or even hundreds, of people and realized you don't know anyone? You're going to have to break the ice, approach strangers, and engage in small talk, and that can give even a major extrovert a case of shyness. The fact that many others in the room are in the same boat doesn't really help the nervousness all that much, does it?

So perhaps you do what I have done many times in my career: you head straight to the bar! You get a drink, and then with that in hand you wind up talking to the first person who makes eye contact or stands in your path. That's fine as far as it goes, and I've met some good contacts that way.

But it's not how spies do it.

The spy's approach is smarter and more economical. Their technique is known as spotting, a strategic way to identify new potential targets for recruitment. This technique and mindset can save salespeople time and enhance their chance at success.

A spy will enter that very same networking event and have a good look around before doing anything else. She is casing out the room and making mental notes about who is there. She flags the silver fox in the center of the group, people gathered around him, making them laugh and holding court. The spy will file that person away, noting that they might be important or influential, but, because they are constantly surrounded by people, they might be difficult to talk to (we'll return to the silver fox in a moment).

The spy will make her way around the room and remember the wallflowers, picking at their hors d'oeuvres—and sipping their drinks. They are a safety zone—she knows that if she needs a quick conversation to keep things flowing, she can always find these introverts, who will be happy to be rescued from their awkwardness.

She will spend time walking through the crowd and taking a look at nametags. She might see a name common to a foreign country she knows well or is interested in. Perhaps she speaks the language. She will note any organizational affinity on a name tag that might present an interesting target.

She will do all this and more before making any approach to anyone at all.

Spotting is a better idea than the beeline to the bar for salespeople who have a limited time in a target-rich environment. Be strategic about who you approach. Remember that you are operating in a particular environment. Whether that is a business cocktail reception around a pool in Miami after a day at a conference, or a law firm breakfast in midtown Manhattan, the atmosphere matters and should consciously inform your approach to developing relationships at the event. Remember the book/cover cliché and to flip it on its head—use what people are advertising about themselves to inform who and how you approach them.

## GO TO WHERE THE CLIENTS ARE

Let's return to the silver fox you've spotted at this cocktail reception. He is clearly someone well connected at this event, and therefore well networked in this particular business community you're interested in. But a good spy knows, as a good salesperson should, that making a pitch in a group is harder than one on one, so trying to get to know that person at this particular event might not be the best approach. You might be able to slip the person a business card and make their acquaintance; but, without the ability to use the tools of influence you've learned, it might not get you that far.

That's where the concept of the access agent comes in. As our spy moves around the room, she is keeping an eye on the silver fox when she's not engaged in discussion with someone (of course, in those conversations, she is using her active listening skills, mirroring behavior, and elicitation techniques). She notes that one person keeps returning to the silver fox. This individual is greeted warmly each time, included in each conversation, and introduces our silver fox to people. This person clearly has the confidence of the silver fox. Seeing that that person is now at the bar, our spy moves in.

Let's say this cocktail reception is taking place at an aerospace conference in Brussels. The reception is crawling with NATO defense contractors, and our spy is a NOC with cover as an aerospace supply-chain consultant.

She introduces herself and uses the skills of social influence to get to know this individual, assessing his personality on the fly and ingratiating herself with him. The conversation is going fairly well, and she focuses entirely on this individual. At one point she hears some loud laughter coming from the group with the silver fox, and she remarks that they seem to be having a good time. Her new contact mentions the name of the silver fox, how he's an old friend and colleague, someone who really likes to enjoy himself and is always the life of the party. Our spy files away his name and the information she's just gotten about her target. After speaking for a while, they exchange cards and agree to get a coffee next week to get to know each other further. She'll meet with this new contact and deepen the relationship until she can credibly find a way to ask for an introduction to the real target—the silver fox.

What she's after is *the warm introduction*, which is the holy grail of espionage or sales. Cold calling is a necessity in sales, but anyone who has done this work for any amount of time understands how valuable it is to be introduced to a target by someone that the target likes and trusts. The chance for success is infinitely higher with someone vouching for you, so it makes sense to develop relationships accordingly.

Access agents have been used by intelligence officers throughout history. John Sipher used access agents regularly in the quest to develop valuable agents. "An access agent could get into a group that I couldn't get into and let me know details to help with my targeting—here is where they like to go to dinner, they have these problems, he plays basketball every Thursday at this location, he loves this bar, etc."

John recounts a particular access agent he ran during the Cold War. That agent had a wide social circle and often would host parties for specific targets—senior communist officials—that John wanted to collect information on or recruit. That agent had a back room in their home where he stored the jackets and other items for his guests as they enjoyed his party. The agent would facilitate John getting access to this storage room, and John would copy keys with a specialized spy gadget and go through their personal items and find notes and other personal details. With the key copies, he and his colleagues could get into their car or house to plant a listening device or collect more information. He might pick up other intelligence about problems in that person's life or find places they frequented.

As a salesperson, or anyone in business, DO NOT rummage through cloakrooms with spy gadgets that copy keys. DO NOT fish through pockets to see if you find receipts or calendars in someone's coat. But DO develop access agents to help you work your way through and/or up the food chain at your target client to find and influence the right person.

Let's go back to the beginning of the book and former CIA Counterterrorism Center chief Bob Grenier's first assignment. Bob got creative on that mission in North Africa to find ways to infiltrate a student communist organization and recruit agents that could help the U.S. government understand this group and whether it presented a threat to U.S. interests. You'll recall that Bob picked up student hitchhikers seeking an entry to the organization. Some of these students became his access agents, ultimately guiding him closer to the leaders of the group.

I had a similar experience when I returned from China to New York and started working in the corporate-security industry. My bosses wanted to grow our business with the financial services community, and part of the appeal of my candidacy for the role I was hired for—beyond my experience in emerging markets, writing and investigative skills, and their assessment of my social skills—was credibility as a true New Yorker. I also had social connections within the financial services industry. Because I grew up in the suburbs of New York and went to college in the Northeast, I came to the job with a network already in place. I knew the type of people who worked in finance.

I was a little wary of this assignment at first. Returning from China, I wanted to live in Brooklyn and spend most of my social time within the arts community (more on that later). I had not been in a fraternity in college, and I didn't necessarily seek social ties with "finance bros."

But I needed to change my mindset. I went out on meetings, lunches, and happy hours with former case officers and watched how they adjusted their personalities to the people they were meeting. On more than a couple of occasions, they shared with me a bit of disdain or disparagement toward the person they were about to meet, but once there you could never tell they felt that way. It seemed to me that they were deeply enjoying or at least happily engaged in all these encounters. I started to realize that doing the same thing was fully within my power. I decided I could go undercover, in a way, to realize my mission of infiltrating the financial-services industry.

One of the first things I did was say *yes* to an invitation for a share-house in the Hamptons. This enclave of villages clustered at the east end of Long Island is known for its beautiful beaches and the wealth of those who spend time there. I knew that by saying yes to that invitation, I would naturally find myself at bars, restaurants, BBQs, pool parties, and beach bonfires with people working in finance. Being a part of a share-house and developing friends in the industry at these parties gave me credibility. Perhaps most importantly, I came with an understanding of this social milieu, having grown up with many of these types of people. I could speak their language.

Over the course of the summer, I met quite a few people in finance, not typically decision-makers, but rather associates, senior associates, and the occasional principal mixed in. They loved hearing all the colorful stories of assignments we worked on in corporate security, and I carefully cultivated these people, employing the tactics I've described in this book, which I was learning in real time from former case officers. These junior members of banks, private equity firms, and hedge funds were able to get me and my colleagues in the door to meet with managing directors and partners at these firms. We successfully pitched many of them and won background investigations, bespoke intelligence gathering projects, executive protection work, and other projects.

I was successful on this mission because I utilized access agents to climb the ladder and get to the decision-makers. I *went to where the clients were*, engaged them, and got to know them in social settings, places where they didn't have their guard up.

Juval Aviv has an interesting take on going to where the clients are. A former officer of the famed Israeli intelligence service, Mossad, Juval was a leader on one of the Mossad's most famous missions: Operation Wrath of God.

This operation was a response to the massacre of eleven Israeli athletes at the 1972 Munich Olympics by affiliates of the Palestinian militant group Black September. As a result of this horrible tragedy, Israel's prime minister, Golda Meir, authorized a years-long mission for the Mossad to track down and kill the planners of the heinous attack.

Juval Aviv would spend nearly five years of his life mostly undercover, tracking down terrorists and bringing them to justice, in Europe and the Middle East. His efforts were memorialized in George Jonas's book *Vengeance* and later by director Stephen Spielberg in his film *Munich*, in which the Eric Bana character is based on Juval.

After the mission ended, Juval settled his young family in the U.S., eager for a change of scenery and new life. Looking to capitalize on the tradecraft and experience he had cultivated in his career so far, he formed Interfor International, a corporate intelligence and security firm (full disclosure—I serve as an advisor to Interfor International).

At this time in the late 1970s, the corporate-security industry was still quite small, but Juval knew he needed a niche. Remember what I noted about how most businesses aren't differentiated by service or price, so salesmanship then becomes a key factor? While that is true, it is also true that finding a niche within an industry can lead to success, and going to where the clients are can be that path forward.

Juval felt that his investigative knowledge and the connections he fostered in the intelligence world and law-enforcement communities could be helpful when it came to the lucrative industry of asset-tracing and bankruptcy rulings. He knew that legal cases around the world often resulted in judgments against defendants who have hidden their assets, and courts often hired outside firms to help locate these assets and assist in recovering them.

To find his niche, Juval studied the industry. He learned that British law is most friendly toward the freezing of cross-border assets, and most aggressive in providing legal cover to penetrate bank secrecy laws. He started to spend a lot of time in the UK, seeking out judges' organizations and pitching himself and his alluring career as a speaker. He found himself giving talks at judicial conferences and getting to know judge after judge. They started to turn to him for help on their cases; and because of Juval's unique skill sets and connections, he delivered. Soon his UK judges began telling their U.S. counterparts about Interfor International and the firm's success in recovering hidden assets.

Juval had gone to where his clients were in the UK, putting himself at their conferences and gatherings, getting to know his targets and cultivating them until work developed. But he also turned those clients into his access agents. When you do good work for people, word gets around, and everyone likes to make a good recommendation. A British judge who makes an introduction for Juval to an American judge feels good about rewarding Juval for his work and building social currency with his counterpart, who will appreciate such a referral.

We can all go to where the clients are, no matter who the clients are. Many of you perhaps already do this. You might play golf at a country club where members of an industry you target are members. That's great, but joining a country club isn't the only way to use this tactic.

What charities are your clients interested in? Sometimes a particular industry has a specific charity that is the focus of support—such as the way hedge funds support the Robin Hood Foundation. But more often, a company will *advertise* the good works they do. Especially in the age of environmental, social, and corporate governance (ESG) and corporate citizenship we're living in, it won't be too hard to find these details. Once you do so, you can get involved in that organization as well, and potentially meet some of your targets (while doing something worthwhile with your time).

Nearly every case officer has stories about joining clubs and organizations during their tours overseas. One told me about his time in the Middle East and how he joined a desert star-gazing club. Get out there, beyond your normal comfort zone, and join different groups, even if they aren't focused on your industry.

I did that when I joined the board of a New York–based non-profit called ISSUE Project Room, New York's leading experimental music center. I was thrilled to be asked to join the board of this influential and deeply important arts organization. But I had no thought about its assisting my career. I was only focused on helping to sustain a venue where I had seen many amazing concerts, and I was excited to have closer access to some of the artists I admired.

But when someone at my office heard that the actor/director Steve Buscemi was on the board, they suggested that our clients would likely love to meet Steve, and perhaps I could set up a dinner.

What followed was a series of dinners and talks that I set up, with Steve's incredibly gracious participation. Steve was an early supporter of ISSUE Project Room, having known its founder, Suzanne Fiol, who tragically had died a few years before my joining the board. Steve felt strongly about continuing the mission of ISSUE Project Room and agreed to have several dinners with investors and speak at events about his fascinating career.

We were able to raise tens of thousands of dollars for ISSUE Project Room that way, and I was able to grow relationships with senior investors who joined these events. The social currency of being associated with such a revered actor also had a great impact on my profile at my company with my colleagues.

Getting creative, getting out of your initial comfort zone, and having passions outside of your career can lead to huge steps forward in your career and personal life. We're going to see how those passions make your life more fulfilling and can offer a chance at serendipity that might just take your career to the next level.

## USE YOUR SUPERPOWERS

Are there a couple of subjects that you feel exceedingly comfortable talking about? These are topics that—if your conversation partner has even the smallest degree of interest—you can discuss with knowledge, dynamism, and personal flair.

Those are your conversational superpowers, and deploying them well when building rapport with a target can help you get to yes.

And it's important to remember that building rapport and deepening a relationship doesn't stop with your initial pitch. *A good case officer re-recruits an asset at every meeting.* You should do the same with your client at every meeting as well, demonstrating to them, beyond your product or service, why they should trust you with their business.

While we're going to dive into three areas that you can cultivate to have better conversations, the first thing to note is that you should *go deep but stay broad*. The idea is that you should strive to have at least three superpowers to have on hand. If you can direct the conversation toward them, you're on solid footing. But staying *broad* will allow you to remain relevant in any conversation, and I have been struck many times by how good former colleagues of mine who are CIA veterans are at using their particular interests and experiences in that way. They seem comfortable, or at least genuinely interested in and curious about, so many different areas.

While I may never be portrayed in a Marvel movie, I'll lay claim to three superpowers and describe how I have used them in impactful ways to develop relationships and make some of the most rewarding sales of my career. I'm very deep with my three superpowers, but I'll admit that I'm not as broad as I would like to be.

You might be thinking, *Listen, Jeremy, it's all well and good that you lived overseas all those years and have all these interesting stories, but that's just not me. I'm a family man, I am involved in my church, I casually watch sports, and I play golf. I don't know if I have three superpowers.*

Never fear! Just as not every case officer is a charming extrovert, not everyone has to have three colorful superpowers in order to master the art of conversation. In fact, listening can be your ultimate superpower, and I would urge you to double down on the attentive-listening techniques we discussed earlier—using your counterpart's words, mirroring their body language, etc. Ace attentive listening, and you don't need to go too deep on other subject matters.

But I would also urge you to consider trying to develop other superpowers. Developing a hobby or an interest will enrich your life and make you more interesting. It will help you connect with people and open new doors that you may never have imagined.

But how to best leverage your superpowers? You might be an avid scuba-diver, but it can seem a pretty random topic to bring up.

It's all about your research. It's essential before attending any conference, prospect meeting, etc., to prepare deeply. Now, the business practices of preparation are distinctive to every organization. Making sure you know everything about your product, how it might be viewed by your target, the competitive landscape, and more—these are all things I'm going to assume you already do as a serious sales pro.

I want you to research the intangibles, the little details that might help you to get to know your target. An analyst in Langley, Virginia, might alert a case officer posted to a third-world country with an administration hostile to U.S. interests that one of their officials has been seen drinking heavily at local bars and there is a rumor that he was passed over yet again for a long-sought promotion. That person is ripe for recruitment. Similarly, maybe your sales-ops team has flagged a company that just had a major supplier issue that has spilled over into a contentious, media-covered legal struggle. Time for you to swoop in and see if you can win the business now that they are on the market.

So you start doing your research, and you find out that the head of procurement is a woman who has been at the company for nearly ten years. She's about your age, and it turns out she went to a college in the Southeast, just as you did. In fact, your schools are rivals, and while you were a junior, her school won the NCAA basketball championship. You're a college basketball nut—it's one of your superpowers—and you know that if she's halfway interested in her college team, you have plenty to connect about.

You see from LinkedIn that she sits on the board of a local animal-shelter charity, and she regularly posts about animal adoption. You and your husband have two dogs you've adopted from a local shelter and feel similarly about the "adopt, don't shop" motto she's regularly posting.

So, while you need to have your game plan together to win the business based on what your company can do for hers, you have two superpower avenues to utilize should there be a chance to mention these connecting details.

You arrive at the client's office and it's a friendly atmosphere; their team—despite the meltdown with their vendor—seems in good spirits. You mirror the somewhat lighthearted mood and mention to your primary target that you're glad she agreed to meet with you, considering you attended a rival school.

"You went where?" she jokes and says she never would have taken the meeting had she known.

You engage in some fun self-deprecating banter about how tough those basketball losses were and how hard it was to watch her team win the championship. But you also mention how much you admire the team, perhaps commenting on the star player's NBA career. Your counterpart is into all of it. She's smiling and making good eye contact. . . . You have started off the meeting well.

Then you continue to crush it, making a solid case about why you should be the new vendor. Things end nicely, and they tell you that they need to consult with colleagues and review your proposal and hope to be back to you in a week or two.

On the way out, you knock on the door of the head of procurement, who walks with you to the lobby. You mention the connection with the pet-adoption cause and talk about the disability one of your dogs has and how challenging but rewarding it has been to care for that dog. *Vulnerability breeds humanity.* You each spend a few minutes sharing some personal thoughts on how family dedication to this cause provides both of you with great meaning and satisfaction in your lives.

You've not only built rapport with an important prospect, but you've deeply connected with another human being. You did your homework and used one of your superpowers to advance your mission.

The thought of a Secret Service agent brings to mind a man in a dark suit, aviator sunglasses, earbud with a wire coil visible from one of his ears, standing quietly in the corner. Stoicism seems to go with the territory for this type of job. But sometimes breaking the Secret Service mold and using a superpower can make you more effective at your job and also foster deep, meaningful lifelong relationships in the process.

Retired Secret Service agent Scott Alswang grew up in a candy store. Sounds like a kid's dream come true, right? But for Scott, growing up with a father who worked in a candy store was largely about economic insecurity. Having done odd jobs since he was a young teenager, Scott was focused on growing his future in the small town of West Orange, New Jersey, being the first of his family to go to college. He finished his undergraduate degree in criminal justice at William Patterson College in the mid-'70s while working 55 hours a week as an armed guard. He joined the police in his hometown, becoming the first Jewish cop in his town's history, and was promoted to detective before leaving to join the Secret Service.

Despite the aforementioned profile of Secret Service agents as taciturn, Scott is anything but. His ebullient personality always drew people to him, and he used it to put protectees and associates at ease. Often charged with pre-planning work at D.C. and New York City hotels for visiting foreign officials, Scott quickly became a favorite of the hotel staffs, which ensured smooth cooperation in keeping everyone safe and happy.

In January 1985, he was working the inauguration for Ronald Reagan after the president's successful reelection campaign. It was one of the coldest inauguration days on record, and much of the ceremony took place inside. Scott was asked to secure an area for VIPs and specifically for Frank Sinatra and his entourage.

When Frank and his wife came through with Don Rickles, the legends introduced themselves to those present and chatted with the team there to support them. Scott was particularly excited to meet Don Rickles, and confessed to him that he had been a fan of his ever since he was a little Jewish boy growing up in New Jersey.

"What's a Jewish kid from New Jersey doing in the Secret Service?"

"Well, sir, I got a master's degree instead of a medical degree."

Don thought this was hilarious, and they continued to banter and chat throughout the day. A friendship formed, one that lasted a lifetime, and Scott was there for Don's funeral in 2017.

When I describe superpowers, it's about particular interests you might have that help you cultivate and influence someone and steer conversations in directions advantageous to you and your mission. Sometimes a superpower is just about an aspect of your personality, like being a great listener. But for Scott it was letting his personality and sense of humor shine through.

This isn't always easy in our professional settings. In even the smallest of teams, a culture forms and we're asked wordlessly to conform to this culture. But the most effective people are those who won't be bound by the expectations of others and can find a way to let their personality and creativity shine while maintaining their professionalism.

Scott's experience of nearly 30 years of public service, including over 20 years in the buttoned-down world of the Secret Service, is an example of that. His winning personality helped facilitate his logistical planning and made him beloved by his protectees. He also put that personality to work overseas, working with his counterparts from similar foreign agencies to form ties that improved cooperation and smoothed the visits of U.S. officials as they traveled abroad.

Scott's work was more effective and more fun because he used the superpowers of his sense of humor and fun personality. Breaking out of molds and finding ways to be your true, most authentic self while being a true professional is something we can all model; and, in doing so, we can aim for what Scott achieved: a rewarding career with deep relationships formed along the way.

My three superpowers: baseball, travel, and music.

Over the course of my career, each one has served me well and enabled me to connect with people quickly, often quite deeply.

I am a baseball fanatic. I got it from my father, who got it from his grandfather, and it's steeped in the history of our team, the New York Yankees. My dad was at Roger Maris's 61st home run, for instance, a little fact that I have trotted out many times for clients when we were bonding about baseball.

I know if I'm at a conference or happy hour, and someone mentions that they are from, say, St. Louis, I will almost certainly say something about the St. Louis Cardinals. If they are remotely interested then, boom, we're off to the races. If I'm traveling to a city not my own, say, Atlanta, and visiting with a prospect or client, it's the same thing—I'll comment on how the Braves' season is going. If I don't get a bite, it's easy enough to move on. If I do, I nearly always come away with a new friend if they have any interest in baseball.

At one of my past jobs, we had season tickets to the Yankees. You might not be surprised to learn I was the most frequent utilizer of the tickets, regularly taking my clients to games. In the early days of spring, I would get messages from these clients, asking when we were going to a game this year. Do you know why that is? Because I'm a fun guy to go to a game with! They enjoyed going with me because I am so genuinely passionate about the sport and my team, and they learned more about baseball by going to games with me. I would try not to be overly didactic, but would point out things about how the players are positioned, or why bunting might make sense here, or a little anecdote about a player; and because I didn't overdo it, and was sincere and excited about it, they responded to that. I knew the concession areas with the best food, where the beer lines were shortest, and the quickest route to the subway as we left the stadium.

While I had this job, my clients were mostly private equity firms; and private equity professionals negotiate for a living. They are notorious for being tough about paying vendors, even at firms with billions of dollars under management. I am absolutely certain that the time I put in with these investors at games helped in our negotiations. I wasn't a counterpart who set out to draw down their dry powder and lower their profit margin: I was *Jeremy*, that awesome dude who takes them out to ballgames where they have a great time.

Travel is another topic I can use to relate to and connect with people. Having lived abroad for almost a decade and traveled widely, it's a subject I know a lot about. Talking about different countries and cultures opens up a vista of different avenues for bonding.

Let's say it's early June. I'm at a conference. It's a coffee break, mid-morning, between sessions. I strike up a conversation with someone as we're filling our mugs, and we chat for a few minutes about the conference and our work. Looking to develop a personal connection, I ask her if she has any travel plans she's excited about for the summer. She mentions that her family has a home in the Adirondacks, where they spend a lot of time during summers. I comment on how beautiful it is up there and she agrees, but mentions how she misses traveling overseas: it's difficult with young kids.

Someone waxing nostalgic about traveling overseas is an invitation for me to use my travel superpower. Within that superpower, I have a special question that I keep ready for such circumstances.

"If you could travel anywhere, where would it be?"

She smiles and says "Well, that's an easy one. It would be Japan. I'm married to a Japanese man and I've never been, if you can believe it. I'd love to visit, and I really want my two kids to learn more about their heritage. I'm also interested in Eastern religions and have wanted to visit the temples in Kyoto for years, even before I met my husband."

I can lean in now and continue to develop the relationship. I've been to Japan several times. I even wrote a story once for *The Japan*

*Times* (on scuba-diving with thresher sharks in the Philippines, of all things). So I'd be able to talk with her about my experience in Japan, just how wonderful those temples in Kyoto are, and a bit about Shinto and Buddhism. We might even get into my shark-diving story: who knows?

You might have also noticed that I asked an elicitation question. Asking about travel dreams didn't only yield an answer to that question, but also gave me bank-shot details about my target that put me in a better position to know her. I know that, in addition to Japan being her dream travel destination, she has young children, is married to a Japanese man, and is interested in Eastern religions. I elicited that all by using the particular question related to one of my three superpowers. I use it all the time in conversation, and it regularly leads to this kind of discovery. People also really enjoy being invited to dream with me about their travel fantasies.

Here's an important caveat when it comes to using your super-powers: using them is not an invitation to grandstand. Do not hop on your soapbox and pontificate about your particular subject of choice. Using your superpowers is about *sharing as a bridge*. Don't lose sight of the fact that it's not about you and ego gratification. I'm not going to say that you should always be the one doing less talking; I'm not creating iron-clad rules of conversation. Sometimes the move could be holding court, being gregarious; sometimes you're on fire, in the zone, and making people laugh and being compelling. If the subject of travel comes up and I mention drinking cobra blood in Taipei or being deported from Brazil (both true stories) and people want to hear more, that's great.

The famed spy novelist John le Carré has described spies as "entertainers." In an interview, he remarked that "most of them have to have entertainment value. Particularly if they are going to recruit people. If I was determined to obtain your services and turn you around and get you to report on your organization, it would be unlikely that you'd agree to come have lunch with me if I weren't a person of some charm and entertainment value." *People remember how you make them feel, and they want to buy from people they like.* Being entertaining and fun to be around is always a good idea.

But using your superpowers isn't just about being fun and entertaining. It's about steering the conversation to places where you can be your best conversationalist and best listener. If I can steer a conversation away from golf—a topic I won't be able to contribute to or (because it bores me) actively listen to—toward one of my superpowers, I can then participate—and I can better gather intel and forge relationships.

Music is a big part of my life—one of my superpowers. I've played guitar since I was thirteen, and I have an active life as a performing and recording musician. I'm interested in all the arts, in fact, and that gives me a broader aperture of connection with a fine point at the center.

Let's say I'm at a meeting in Chicago. There are a bunch of clients sitting with me in a conference room, but one woman stands out. I notice her funky hairstyle, glasses with chunky frames, maybe a tattoo or two (or seven) peeking out from a sleeve or neckline; maybe it's just intuition and the type of vibes I'm registering.

The meeting ends, so I take the opportunity to chat with this woman on the sidelines. I mention that I'm a big music fan, that my taste tilts a bit more experimental, and I'm wondering whether she has any suggestions for shows while I'm in town tonight. I've used the opposite of the book/cover cliché to plan my approach and gambled that she's the kind of person who shares these musical interests with me.

Perhaps she asks me a bit more about what I'm into. I describe some of the music I've been listening to, artists I have seen lately, and I see her eyes broadening, a small smile developing, and body language turning positive and open. She tells me she loves one of the artists I mentioned, and she saw another one of my favorites when they were passing through Chicago a few weeks ago. She recommends a few venues to check out, even mentions that she's going to a show tonight with friends if I want to join.

Or maybe she shrugs her shoulders and doesn't have much to add. It turns out she isn't a big music fan. It's a swing and miss, but did I hurt anything? Would she take offense at my asking her these questions? Not likely; so its minimal downside and high upside make it a good bet to take this kind of approach. If it's that first scenario, where we've connected about music, I have developed an ally within my client organization. Even if she's not the decision-maker and holds limited sway on the team, she can be my access agent feeding me inside information, organizational changes, and all the scuttlebutt within her team.

Remember the spy who skied? How he needed to get creative to find a way to connect with Russian diplomats in Central Asia to help collect intelligence on Russia during a critical moment at the end of the Cold War?

As we discussed early on, it's unlikely that Rick* thought his love of skiing would lead to one of the most important agent recruitments of his career. But that's what using your superpowers can bring you. If you follow your passion(s), you will find that hidden doors open up.

Let me tell you about how my baseball superpower led to the biggest professional highlight of my career.

Years ago, I was at a business networking event, and I was using some of the spotting skills I'd learned from case officers. Not long before this day, I would have made my way around the room less strategically, talking to whoever crossed my path, as I've described. But I had a plan now, and as I cased the room for targets I noticed a man with a label saying he worked for the New York Yankees. He had a senior security role with the organization, and he reacted well to my initial approach. We really hit it off when I expressed interest in his job, and he was charmed by my love of the Yankees.

A professional friendship developed, and he invited me up to the stadium for a tour. My new friend took me on the field and into the clubhouse. But it was only a start.

Not long afterward, he called me to inquire if my security firm could brief the team on some of the security issues that the players face.

A large portion of Major League players come from countries like Venezuela, the Dominican Republic, Mexico, and other Latin American countries where there are significant security issues. Players from these countries are high-profile targets, earning many times more than the average citizen, and they are huge celebrities in these baseball-mad countries. So players and their families have unfortunately been the target of criminals bent on robbery, kidnapping, and extortion.

In February 2016, I partnered with a bilingual colleague to brief the team in Spanish and in English on a variety of ways to manage and mitigate risks, including how to think about their usage of social media, always keeping safety in mind.

Ending the second session, my colleague pointed over at me as he concluded his talk with the assembled players. I was just standing on the sidelines in a suit, doing my best to affect gravitas even though I felt like my ten-year-old self in the room with my favorite team. My colleague said "... and Jeremy Hurewitz is a New York–based security consultant. You should get a card from him and keep it handy. Give him a call if you have anything at all you want to discuss concerning the safety of you and your families."

All the players, athletes I revered, looked over at me like I was some kind of elite spy or Navy SEAL. I gravely nodded at them, betraying nothing, all business. . . .

It was the start of a lucrative, revenue-recurring relationship with one of the world's most valuable sports franchises. That, of course, is incredibly valuable on its own. But the day means even more to me than that. It's one of the best days in my career. I was in that inner circle with my beloved New York Yankees, with team management and the players hanging on every word that my colleague and I had to share about their safety. All because I'd followed my passion and leveraged one of my superpowers.

A key lesson of using your superpowers is, of course, to find the subjects you can count on to have better conversations, to help you break through awkward moments, to help move conversations from subjects you find dull to areas you're passionate about and can shine when discussing and activating your best active listening skills.

But the hidden beauty of developing and deploying your superpowers is the sheer enjoyment you can get from interests beyond your career. A life with passions is richer, and unexpected avenues open to you when you have such a life. So, dig in on those areas in your own life, and if you have an incipient interest in something—Thai cooking, rock climbing, gardening, whatever it is—lean into those things. Your life and career will be better for it.

## "CRAWL, WALK, RUN"

It's hard to give someone a relationship-building playbook. One of the reasons I developed the *Sell Like a Spy* program was in response to rigidly programmatic sales trainings I attended. They took a formulaic approach to business development that I found stultifying. I'm not saying that I got nothing out of these sales trainings, but let's say it was close to nothing. Perhaps someone new to sales would benefit from some of these sessions I had to sit through. But I was a bit further along in my career and found what was being taught to be confining. For me, sales is more of an art than a science, and efforts to turn it more into the latter left me cold. It certainly took the fun and creativity out of sales. Some of the people doing the teaching, and indeed some of the so-called sales gurus I see regularly on LinkedIn and elsewhere with their data-focused approach, have never actually sold anything and are highly awkward people in social settings. Give me a case officer who has spent years growing a wide variety of relationships with difficult assets all over the world over a script-reliant sales rep any day of the week.

So, while the *Sell Like a Spy* program is not a playbook—*do X to get to Y*—I have come across a case-officer-development method called "Crawl, Walk, Run" that is a useful philosophy to study, especially for landing that big fish. As with any development method that recognizes sales as an art, there is plenty of room to customize it and make it your own. It's a loose idea of how to engage that bigger potential client with patience and focus.

The case officer who told me about this method would start the process of developing a target, but take his time getting to know that person: *Crawl.*

As he evaluated the target, they began the dance of relationship development together. He would learn about what was important to the target, what made that person tick, whether they had redlines and vulnerabilities that he had to keep in mind to get this person to cooperate with him. They had started *Walk*ing together on the path to espionage.

Once that relationship was established and he felt he knew what the target needed; once he felt he was likely to get a yes, then it was time to *Run*—make the offer and be fearless about it. "*Get people to come along slowly, and then all at once,*" is the idea he told me, with a wink.

I'm going to share a "Crawl, Walk, Run" example from my sales career. The strategy was so effective, in this case, that the result proved to be the biggest sale of my career.

I was an ambitious business-development professional at a consulting firm, one with a great and supportive culture but also a demanding, competitive quota structure.

Scouring our CRM system for hidden gems, I came upon a middle-market private-equity firm that was ostensibly based in New York, where I was located, but had all the rest of its operations in several Asian offices, where it focused all its investment.

Supported by our Hong Kong office, this firm paid mine around $100k annually for research services, and that hadn't changed much in the last few years.

I noted from its website that the founder of the firm, its CFO, another investment professional, and a few back-office types were in New York. I learned from his bio that the founder of the firm was an experienced investor in the Asia/Pacific region and a member of the Council on Foreign Relations (CFR) one of the premier foreign policy think tanks in the U.S. And I had been to many events at the CFR townhouse on the Upper East Side of Manhattan.

I took a chance and sent the founder a message, noting that I had background in Asia as well and asking if he would be open to having a chat with me. I mentioned that I thought there was more our firm could do for him, especially specifically in New York.

I got a bite—he quickly responded that he would be happy to meet.

At the meeting, we had an immediate rapport. Down-to-earth and intellectually curious, Steve* was a pleasure to talk to. He appreciated hearing about my background and respected my strongly held views on China's role in the world and other aspects of Asia and economics.

I mentioned to Steve that my firm occasionally hosted what we called "elite events" with some of the top names in New York finance, matched typically with a top former government official. These included former heads of the Defense Department, Treasury, CIA, and other top-level cabinet officials. These were marquee names, and so were the clients of ours who sat at the table of generally less than a dozen people total, a veritable "who's who" of New York finance. Would he be interested in joining for such an event?

Steve perked up. Though he didn't strike me as particularly egotistical—which is all relative in the upper echelons of finance— he was clearly excited about the prospect.

I realized that Steve had an unfulfilled emotional need as our client—*he wanted a seat at the table*. I was able to deliver that to him. We had started Crawling together.

Remember when I noted how important it was to develop relationship equity with other members of your team, beyond specifically the sales team? Because I was friendly with the folks who helped with our presentations, they did me a solid when I needed it, quietly pushing my PowerPoint decks to the top of the queue and going the extra mile to make sure they popped. I was similarly friendly with the events team; and while seats at the elite events were hard to get and I had to petition the head of sales as well as the head of events, they could tell I was hunting big game and gave me what I needed.

Over the next couple of months, I would get Steve to some of the most sought-after events at our firm, which were some of the most valued events in New York for this stratum of people. I also arranged private visits for Steve with other top foreign-policy wonks and economists, often accompanying these figures to his office, letting the two of them do nearly all the talking, but chiming in occasionally to hold my own and establish myself as something of an intellectual peer and not just a functionary.

I realized that despite how much Steve was enjoying all these meetings, we needed to paint a broader picture of what our firm could do for his investment team if I was going to complete my mission. I drew further on the relationship equity I had developed with coworkers and brought in senior colleagues on several occasions to help describe the deeper level of support our firm could provide, making them more efficient, and, most importantly, more successful.

We were Walking.

A sidebar on leveraging colleagues: I know a decent amount about a few subjects, and I have a passion for relationship development. But, of course, I don't know everything, and throughout my career I have regularly leaned on colleagues with specialized knowledge of my firm's services or policy areas. I would also regularly bring in the most senior members of my firm, up to and including my CEO, for the right client opportunity. The bottom line is that we are a society that respects hierarchy, and that is particularly true in New York City's finance world.

Salespeople have frequently surprised me with a resistance to leveraging others in their pitches. Maybe it's ego or a desire to be constantly in control, but they want to be the star of the show and don't take enough advantage of leveraging expertise or senior management.

Bringing in senior leaders at your company can be a risky proposition. What if the meeting doesn't go well or you simply don't perform well? Some salespeople might not want to take the risk, but that hasn't stopped me. The upside has always been worth it, both with the client and with leadership, especially if I performed as I had expected I would and was proud of the relationship I had established with the client.

After a few months of courtship with Steve, the time came to make the ask. I was particularly pleased that I had held back from being the one to raise the question of a price tag for the expanded relationship I had been developing. I had been enjoying getting to know Steve, tagging along on many of the fascinating conversations. But despite the fact that I was enjoying the process, this patience isn't always indicative of my approach. Being a New Yorker and always in a hurry, I had to hold my own reins and practice patience as our walking pace picked up.

We were ready to Run, and I had the starting gun in hand.

Debriefing after his latest visit with a foreign-policy leader, Steve reflected on how much he had been enjoying the last few months and getting to know my firm's expanded offerings. But he wondered what the type of relationship I had been demonstrating to him would cost his firm if he wanted to take that step.

I had been preparing for that moment, but felt some butterflies in my stomach as it happened. So much of my work for the last few months was now on the line. I took a deep breath and replied, "Well, Steve, firms like yours are typically paying us around a million dollars and up annually for this type of deep relationship and access."

And then I waited. I was tempted to say "but, you know, if that is too much, we can surely figure out something that works," worried that I would blow him out of the water with a price tag ten times what he was currently paying and jeopardize my mission and months of work. But I had developed a conviction—through research and preparation—that I should start at this number. And remember, one of the most important rules of sales is *don't negotiate against yourself.*

After a moment that felt like an eternity, Steve replied "Well, I'm not quite sure we can get there exactly, but I'm interested in exploring more."

I was excited. I had started with a very high price tag and Steve wasn't outraged. He knew where we were, and as an experienced negotiator himself he knew he was going to have to pay handsomely for this level of support. I wasn't quite sure where this race would lead, but I was confident it was to somewhere good.

We ultimately landed at $750k, a 650 percent increase on what they were paying year-over-year. It was at the time the second largest upgrade in the history of my decades-old firm, and it was one of the largest and most admired deals that year, garnering much talk around the watercooler and praise for yours truly.

The benefits to me were huge. Steve, who had at this point enormous trust in me, wanted my firm to send me to Asia to meet with his partners and brief them on our new, deeper relationship. I had a fantastic trip to Singapore and Hong Kong. I was promoted to vice president and given a prestigious speaking spot at the firm's annual conference, closing out the multi-day event with my description of closing the big deal. Perhaps most importantly, depending on how you value these things, it led to a quota-busting bonus.

All because I followed the "Crawl, Walk, Run" development strategy. I targeted a firm and a founder that I thought was underserved and to whom I could be a particularly good partner. I listened and observed carefully and discovered an emotional need in my target that wasn't being met. I leveraged the internal equity I had at my firm through diligent relationship management, which the many arrogant sales professionals on my team surely noted, perhaps reconsidering the condescending ways they treated those who supported our work. And I successfully executed the "Crawl, Walk, Run" playbook, being patient when I needed to, and bold when it was time to start the race.

## KEY TAKEAWAYS

Disguises and cover stories are real aspects of spy tradecraft, not Hollywood fictions, and we can take inspiration from these espionage methods to bring out the best sides of our personalities to meet the moment. We can also leverage spy-development techniques in creative networking, strategic usage of "warm introductions," and patient relationship growth to achieve your mission and make that sale.

1.   Network like a spy! Use the spotting technique to be strategic about who you talk to and how you approach them.
2.   Get in the habit of developing "access agents" to help you reach the influential contact you covet or to gain insight into a target organization you're looking to penetrate.
3.   Go to where the clients are to meet potential sales targets in an environment where they don't have their professional armor up. Get creative and become iconic!
4.   Use your superpowers to have better conversations, to put yourself in a position to be a great active listener, and to welcome serendipitous opportunities that could change your life.
5.   Use the "Crawl, Walk, Run" method to patiently develop that big prospect. Understand your target's emotional needs and don't negotiate against yourself.

# AFTERWORD

We all know that there is promise and peril in technology. We walk around during our everyday lives with supercomputers in our pockets, gadgets that contain access to all human knowledge. But we all also understand the way technology has ushered in an era of acute divisiveness via social media and the echo chambers it has forced us into. The way we talk past each other, making little effort to try to understand each other, is one of humanity's biggest current challenges.

Technology-based silos are evident in corporate culture, as well. My career and life experience reflect a restless spirit, an intellectual curiosity, and a desire to try new things and confront different challenges. My varied experiences and interests, I thought, would make companies take notice when I applied for certain jobs, despite not having worked in those particular fields. Fresh perspectives, new approaches, . . . that's what I was bringing to the table. Maybe I had a couple of the requirements for a job, along with a strong interest in the role. I would write a killer cover letter describing my qualifications and what I could uniquely bring to the job.

Then, I'd find myself scratching my head after not even getting a first interview. What I didn't know then but clearly understand now is the increased usage of artificial intelligence in human resources departments. And as I noted earlier in this book, AI is quite adept at screening out people who don't have the very particular skill sets or experience a company is looking for. You could write the greatest cover letter in history, but the qualitative side of the job search seems to get thrown out the window as the computer programs filter out applicants who don't fit a narrow profile.

Science writer David Epstein references this phenomenon in his excellent book, *Range*. He notes how the trend has hurt what he calls "serial innovators" and how it encourages "hyper-specialization." Citing the research of sociologists to back up what is by now an obvious point in corporate culture, he explains that people with wide-ranging experiences are getting screened out because "their breadth of interests do not neatly fit a rubric." He quotes innovation-management expert Abbie Griffin and her co-researchers, writing that "a mechanistic approach to hiring, while yielding highly reproducible results, in fact reduces the numbers of high-potential candidates." At this point in his book Epstein has shown how "serial innovators" and others who might be considered "outsiders" in a certain field often have some of the most creative ideas about how to solve problems.

To bring it back to the spy world, if a case officer was to leave the Agency and apply for a corporate sales job, she or he would likely be immediately screened out as lacking the necessary experience and skill set. This would happen even though, as I have hopefully shown in this book, spies are in fact the world's best salespeople.

I have been thinking about the concepts underpinning *Sell Like a Spy* for many years, since some of my earliest experience working with former intelligence officers as we collaborated in the corporate security world. But I was also driven to develop these concepts and this book while sitting through quite a few corporate sales trainings, which I noted earlier in the book are reflective of this drift toward a mechanistic approach to achieving corporate goals.

These trainings were overly mechanistic themselves, turning sales from what I know is an art into what they want you to believe is a science. Do A to get to B, you're instructed, with no sense that there are actually many paths to get from A to B, or to get from initial outreach to closing a deal. Listen, I get that many people, especially those early in their careers, can benefit from learning, for instance, how to write a cold outreach email. But making people feel like coloring within a certain set of lines will make them successful and that not doing so will lead to failure just isn't correct. Furthermore, it drains what should be a deeply human and even fun process of creativity and enjoyment. Who enjoys reproducing a series of rote tasks?

Many of these trainings, and much of what I read in books and many (many) LinkedIn posts by supposed sales experts are from data nerds who are often deeply lacking in social skills. *"Studies have shown that sending an outreach email to your prospect on a Thursday afternoon between 2–4 PM will increase your chance of a reply by 23 percent!"* If this is helpful to you, that's great, but that is not how I was able to find sales success, and it is certainly not how spies are able to achieve their unique form of sales success.

Every skill and strategy I have described in this book is meant as a jumping-off point for you to make it your own. If you're someone who uses a lot of your own body language when you speak, you shouldn't lose that trait when you're interacting with someone, whether you're trying to mirror their behavior or elicit information. You might decrease your body language a bit, but standing statue-still because I wrote that you should calm yourself to be a good active listener will just make you seem awkward. What's in this book and at the heart of these lessons is how to be particular versions of yourself (because, as we've seen, we all have multitudes) and to understand a bit more about human behavior to leverage that best side of your humanity to connect deeply.


The world of technology, of course, has also profoundly impacted how espionage is conducted. For every benefit that technology brings to spy development in areas like electronic eavesdropping for the development of a spy sales lead (an intercepted email reveals a diplomat has a sick child that can't get proper care in their home country), the spy faces just as many if not more hurdles in our tech-infused world. Facial recognition software—increasingly ubiquitous, especially in many authoritarian countries—has made the work of clandestine agents increasingly difficult and pushed the boundaries of disguise tradecraft. With the internet available across the globe, a spy must now have a detailed cover story and likely stick to it throughout their career, whereas it used to be that a spy might be able to operate with official and non-official cover at different points in their career.

Despite these technological developments and the challenges that they bring, spies still operate firmly within the realm of "the human palette" as Bob Grenier put it in the foreword to this book. Even with advantages that they now have when looking to develop a relationship by knowing so much more than in the past about a target's life, they must still use their very human skills to elicit information, listen effectively, mirror behavior to build rapport, and use empathy, even when dealing with some very bad people.

It is my hope that you as a reader who navigates our modern world—where technological currents seem to push us into narrow eddies that form social groups, where we are increasingly bucketed into confined career paths—you might use what these exceptional professionals use to break out of these confines and define your own world and career. By leaning into your superpowers and developing new ones, by cultivating intellectual curiosity, and by taking inspiration from how spies and other remarkable government professionals work with that human palette, you might find your own unique and rewarding path toward success and fulfillment.

## ACKNOWLEDGMENTS

One of the nicer conventions in modern American society is thanking military members for their service. In an all-volunteer military, it's a small gesture of gratitude offered to someone who has made sacrifices for their country.

Because members of the military can be identified by their uniform, it can be easy to spot them and offer such thanks. Spies are a different story; there is no uniform for intelligence officers. Yet members of the intelligence community—along with members of the FBI, Secret Service, and other government agencies—have also bravely served their country, often in dangerous situations. They are no less worthy of gratitude.

It is a great honor to be able to shine a spotlight on these individuals with this book, and I want to thank them for their service and share how much I admire them (though it should already be evident to readers of *Sell Like a Spy*). I hope that this book has played a role in reframing the work these people do from the fantasy world of Hollywood to the true reality where they operate, which is honestly no less extraordinary.

I want to thank the individuals I was able to name in this book, and the many more whom I was not, both for their service and for their willingness to share their time and expertise with me. I wish to thank Bob Grenier in particular. As Bob noted in his foreword, I approached him with the concept of *Sell Like a Spy* and he was instantly supportive, immediately understanding the connections I was making, and enthusiastically lending his support and knowledge to what I was building. He has become a friend and mentor, and I am forever grateful for him sharing his expertise and time with me.

I had the great honor of learning directly from Steve Romano and Gary Noesner in the past. Steve, in particular, has spent a lot of time helping me understand how the FBI utilizes "skills of social influence." Steve has not only been a tremendous source of information and inspiration for this book, but he has also been a valuable and sagacious voice offering a valuable perspective on the troubled political landscape of America in its current dysfunctional season.

I have traveled many paths in my career and have had the good fortune of learning from some amazing people, some of whom I reference in this book, and others I don't. I wish to thank a few of those as well.

Perhaps no one has had a greater influence on my career than my friend, mentor, and former boss, Professor Andrzej Rapaczynski. Andrzej and I played a large part in building Project Syndicate into the influential international media organization it is today, and I learned so much about business and the world in that process. I also learned what it's like to be a compassionate leader who is willing to listen to smart ideas, wherever they might come from. Thank you, Andrzej, for all that you have done for me.

Michael Cullen gave me my first shot in the corporate security world and helped me find my legs in the industry, all while having a good time doing so. Pat Donegan is mentioned in the book, but I wish to thank him here as well for the big role he played in deepening my sales acumen and shaping my views on team building and leadership. Huge thanks to Theresa Boyce of CEO Trust and Sarah Hunt of the Joseph Rainey Center for Public Policy, as well as Sam Jacobs of Pavilion, Edmund Green, Gary Anzalone, and Greg Monaco for their collaboration and support.

I'm deeply grateful to my colleagues at Interfor International for their support. The executive team of Ben Kunde, Daniel Zaffran, and Tom Suozzo are a top-notch group, and I continue to grow professionally through our collaborative work. I'm particularly grateful to Don Aviv, President of Interfor International, for involving me in the fascinating work that the firm does. Combining professionalism and high-quality work with a commitment to its people is not something every firm gets right, but Interfor is consistently successful in threading the needle on that difficult assignment.

I'm incredibly lucky to have great friends who have supported me in the process of developing *Sell Like a Spy*. First in that group is Daniel Levine, a multi-decade friend whose successful career in public speaking informed all these efforts. Daniel has gone the extra mile in helping me shape nearly everything I've done on this project, and I'll always be grateful to him for it. Daniel, along with Geof Rochester, Lari Konfidan, Andy Albeck, and Anastasia Trifonoff, listened to an early practice talk of mine and helped shape what was to come. Jarrod Yahes's friendship over 40-plus years and his early support for this idea have meant a lot. Greg Walters, Brian Bowman, Geoff Green, Carl Porcaro, and Kevin Human are a few other important friends who have supported me on this journey, though there are others that I will inevitably regret not including. I wish to thank them as well.

Big thanks to my friend Elise Ballard for introducing me to my agent, Michael Signorelli of Aevitas Creative Management. Michael's guidance and collaboration with this first-time author was huge for me, and I'm immensely grateful for his belief in this project early on. I'm looking forward to the future, Michael.

The team at Diversion Books has been incredible in developing this book and I have been inspired by their enthusiasm for it. I wish to thank my editor Keith Wallman and editorial assistant

Clara Linhoff for their work with me on it. Thank you for making the process fun and collaborative.

My family has been behind me through the different iterations of my career. A highlight for me in this book is mentioning the social gifts my parents possess and how I have learned so much from them. But well beyond that, they are simply the most wonderful and loving people anyone could hope to have as parents, and I'm deeply thankful for them. My sister, Jessica Mandler; her husband, Brian; and their two kids, Emily and Mason, have been incredibly supportive, and my love for them knows no bounds. Thanks to my English professor mother-in-law, Jo Ellen Winters, for her literary and moral support. I wish to thank the rest of my extended family, who are a warm and loving group that I'm lucky to have in my life.

At the heart of everything is my incredible wife, Rachel Winters, who has stood by me through thick and thin on our fun and unique journey together. Without Rachel, I doubt this book would have seen the light of day. And she brings that light to my world every day. My gratitude and love for Rachel are endless.